**People Stories
In 600 Words
As told by a raconteur**

Written by Elliot M. Rubin

People Stories in 600 Words
As told by a raconteur
First edition

Copyright August 3, 2010 by Elliot M. Rubin
Library of Congress registration #TXu001709645
ISNB # 099130604X

No part of this book may be reproduced in any form whatsoever without prior, express written consent of the author.
This book is fiction and all names, people, places and happenings are from the author's imagination and are used fictionally.
Any resemblances to any living or dead persons, and/or businesses, locations and/or events are coincidental in its entirety.

All rights reserved.

Acknowledgements

　　I would like to thank my late father, Herman S. Rubin, for his inspiration and his sense of humor.
　　He wrote essays, prayers, and poetry his whole life and his writings are treasured by those who have read them.
　　As to his sense of humor my youngest daughter was five when he died. She asked if he died from laughing too much. What a pleasant way to be thought of.
　　And lastly, and most importantly, I want to thank my dear wife, Laura, for her keen disinterest that kept driving me to write more.

People Stories in 600 Words
As told by a raconteur
By Elliot Rubin

Introduction

One day I was driving on the New Jersey Garden State Parkway listening to National Public Radio and they were reading three minute short stories that people had submitted to the station.

The host was reading them and said they were about 600 words in length and as people would send them in she would read them on air.

I started to think that I could do that.

Everyone wants to write the great American Novel but I usually write in a very concise manner.

I thought that this is the perfect vehicle for me so I started to write these short 600 word stories. In a sense it is very much like haiku in that there are parameters to stay within. These types of short stories are called Flash Fiction and have to be between 500 and 1,000 words.

My stories are about people and all are at or near the 600 word parameter I set for myself. In most of the stories there is somewhere deep inside a figment of reality and truth.

They are human beings with all their foibles and traits. Life is interesting that way, never exactly as we would like it, just happening.

On occasion it just seems to go in circles with no point at all.

Sometimes the endings are not what we thought they should be, or like.

Any actual names or events used are purely coincidental and are not done on purpose.

I have also taken some creative liberties in writing as these are all fiction short stories.

To fully enjoy this book it is **STRONGLY** suggested that after each story you _wait_ a moment or so and think about the people you just read about.

This type of book is not meant to be read through page after page, but digested like a fine meal and appreciated slowly. Thank you

Introduction 4
1 - Carmen 7
2 - California..9
3 – Annie Armstrong 11
4 - Atlantic Beach 13
5 – The Rabbi 15
6 - Selma..17
7 - Frankie 19
8 – The Funeral 21
9 - Patsy...23
10 - Bernard...25
11 - The Bakery...27
12 - Keisha 29
13 - Bart...31
14 – The Bar..33
15 - Carl...35
16 – Abby 37
17 – Tar Beach..39
18 - Casino 41
19 – Summer at Blue Meadow Lake 43
20 - Moses 45
21 – The Back Window..47
22 – A Gift...49
23 – Visiting Virginia..51
24 – Gypsy Girl...53
25 - Daria...55
26 – Drug Bust 57
27 – Newlyweds 59
28 – The Airplane 61
29 – A Nun's Story..63
30 – NYC Councilman 65
31 - Ella 67

32 - Juan	69
33 - Andrea	71
34 - Alone	73
35 - Shanice	75
36 – K.A.C. Crib	77
37 - Dad	79
38 - Aliens	81
39 – Las Vegas	83
40 – New	85
41 - Suzanne	87
42 – The Bridge	89
43 - Izzi	91
44 – Rabbi Darke	93
45 – The Bank	95
46 - Life	97
47 – O Called	99
48 - Politics	101
49 – Aunt Betty	103
50 – Seaside Grove	105
51 – The Shop	107
52 – In-Home Service	109
53 – Mary the Teller	111
54 – Life in Ancient Israel	113
55 – Karla	115
56 – Lebanon	117
57 - Todd	119
58 - Voices	121
59 - A Final Goodbye	123
60 - NASA	125
61 – The Date	127
62 – High School	129
63 - Cheryl	131

65 - Blanche I 135
66 – Blanch II 137
67 – Blanch III 139
68 – The Last Kiss 141
69 – The Draft 143
70 – The Actress 145
71 – The Detail 147
72 - Phyllis 149
73 - Brooklyn 151
74 - The Other Woman 153
75 – Unrequited 155

1 - Carmen

As Carmen walked slowly up the steps in front of the church, she had many thoughts racing through her mind.

How would she start; what should she say first? It wouldn't be easy for her to talk about her troubled marriage.

She was dressed conservatively. After all she was entering a holy place and that was how she was raised. Her mother and grandmother wore only black after their husbands had died. They never dated or even thought of doing so.

Yet here she was about to talk to the priest about a marriage in free fall. She thought she had tried her best to make it work. They were married for five years and only after the first six months did she discover the secret her husband had kept from her and never told her. And she never told him hers either.

Slowly she opened the large wooden doors that every church has in Brooklyn. It seems the bigger the doors, the larger the church. They were well oiled and they opened easily as she walked into the cool, darkish vestibule. The only light was from the skylight above her. But she could see just ahead the rows of candles burning in the front of the church.

The church office was in the rear and as she walked down the center of the church she looked up. The ceiling was so high it seemed it almost touched heaven.

Perhaps Jesus would hear her story and help her. She had nowhere to turn, or no one to turn to, except for Father Donovan.

Carmen was in her late twenties and had very soft features. Her olive skin and her small thin-lipped mouth didn't betray the fact she was of Italian heritage. Not like her older sisters who were big boned, had fuller mouths and were very loud, outgoing women.

She was a petite girl and carried herself well. Dark black hair tied back into a ponytail. She rarely let it down except at night when she went to bed. That was because her husband had requested that. He liked her with her hair down.

When she opened the doors to Father Donovan's office she saw him sitting behind his desk reading the newspaper.

He had been an athlete when he was younger, before he had a calling for the priesthood.

The toned muscles were still there as he went to the parish gym every day. Chiseled facial features foretold the tight abdomen beneath his black jacket and starched white collar.

Carmen entered and apologized for being a little late. Her mother came downstairs before she left and started a conversation with her. She didn't dare tell her mother where she was going, and why.

When she entered, her eyes caught his and they looked at each other. There were unspoken words communicated between them by their gaze.

He dared not say what he thought, nor would she.

Carmen sat down in the faded, crinkled brown leather chair that was in front of his desk.

How could she tell him her thoughts, her desires? How can she even begin speaking of her marriage when she had these unholy feelings?

Father Donovan broke the silence and mentioned how nice the weather was. Spring had finally come to Brooklyn and the flowers were blooming. A new start to life was happening outside. Yet inside the church, flowers of a marriage were wilting.

Finally he outstretched his arm and gently held her hand. Softly she started to talk.

Carmen was confident that she was protected. The secret in her marriage would not be betrayed.

It is suggested that after each story you *wait* a moment or so and think about the people you just read about before going on. Thank you.

2 - California

I was riding my red Harley Davidson special edition Firefighter Fat Boy along the Pacific Coast Highway with the sound of the breaking waves to my right and the roar of the mighty engine between my legs. The air smelled of salt water with the morning sun beating down on my face.
Ecstasy.
Her chest was pushed firmly into my back as she held her arms tightly around my waist while I gently turned the bike in on the curves. She had blond hair and it was blowing in the wind trailing behind us on our journey.
The skintight tee shirt she was wearing was stretched to its maximum as we sped along enjoying the day.
Utopia must be like this. Not a care in the world. No work stress, no nagging spouse, no monthly mortgage payments to make or worry about.
She had packed a bag lunch and it was in the saddlebags that were astride the rear fenders.
We saw a small general store in a local town and we stopped to get something cold to drink while we rested and ate the lunch she had packed.
I watched her as she put the bottle to her luscious lips and slowly drank, enjoying each gulp with a calm satisfaction.
She retired from modeling a few years ago and was living off her savings. Her face appeared on many magazine covers over the years. But at thirty-nine, she was considered over the hill.
The fashion world discarded her like yesterday's news.
She still had her shape and had even improved with age. A little fuller but she still was a knockout with curves in all the right places. Not model skinny anymore, just packed firmly into a wonderful sight to behold.
Yet here I was with her. What did I do to deserve this?

Having grown up in Brooklyn, I never would have imagined me here at this time in my life. So far from the hustle and bustle of Flatbush Avenue, the crowds in Manhattan, the smell of pollution stagnating in the air during the 1960s.

My mind flashed back to the girls I dated when I was in high school.

They were nice girls, some more fun than others. Yet they didn't compare to her. They were skinny, some had a little more weight on them, some were smaller, but they were teenagers and so was I. Acne and all the other problems of teenagers.

Yet here I was in California with the woman of my dreams. Probably she was the woman of many men's dreams. High cheek bones, long flowing blonde hair, and pink full lips you could die for.

When we were finished eating she leaned over to me and gently pursed her lips as she softly pressed them to mine. She whispered in my ear the loving words I had desired to hear from her. Life could not get any better.

We got back on the Harley and I pushed the clutch in, kicked the pedal down into first, gave it some gas and we took off again with her holding onto me tightly.

Then I smelled something I didn't before.

Traffic had started again and I was passing the Kill Van Kull in Staten Island going to work in my Chrysler family van.

Reality struck me.

Back to Brooklyn and the wonderful journey I had just taken was gone as fast as it began.

It is suggested that after each story you *wait* a moment or so and think about the people you just read about before going on. Thank you.

3 – Annie Armstrong

The funeral was very sad. She was only twenty-eight years old. An innocent bystander caught in a mindless drug war between two gangs. She was just talking to friends when a stray bullet found her.

Annie Armstrong was only six years old when I first met her. She was very short for her age and was not particularly good looking. But there was an inner beauty about her. She had a peaceful aura that when you really looked at her you saw a pretty face. Someone might even say she was cute looking but in a different kind of way.

She wore either pigtails or corn rows every day and her mother dressed her in colorful dresses for school.

She lived in a rundown area of Jersey City and attended the neighborhood elementary school. The principal would go into his office every day, lock the door, and not come out until three o'clock. This was the "old school" principal who did not relate to black children and was way past his prime.

He came into the system thirty years before when the school was white and Irish/Italian. He could not relate to these black children of poverty, although the white students before them were not any better off.

Annie was an average student and as she got older, she helped her mother at home cleaning and doing the dishes. She even started to learn how to sew.

When she was in middle school she took a sewing class for a year and was really good at it. She started to make her own clothes and wear them to school. They were very different and colorful.

Against her very dark skin the clothes just jumped out at you. They were stylish and even *avant garde*. The other kids took notice.

By the time she got into high school Annie was designing, making, and selling her clothes to other students. Her mother worked at night cleaning offices and warehouses so she could support Annie and herself.

Annie's money helped her mother take it easy. She was able to quit her night job and only worked during the day cleaning at a nearby office building.

One day Annie was shopping in Journal Square when a lady came up to her and asked where she bought her clothes. She thought they were very unique and she was a fabric cutter for a boutique clothing factory in Manhattan. She thought her boss might be interested in Annie's designs.

Annie explained that she made her own clothes and the lady gave her a card to call. It was a famous clothing designer in the city that she worked for. She would pass the word along so they should expect her call.

That night Annie told her mother what had happened and she was so excited.

Maybe this was the way out of the city for her and her mother.

The call was made, a meeting set up, and her designs were met with unexcelled delight.

A new clothing line was going to be produced based on Annie's designs. A billboard was planned for Times Square and a very large advance was paid to Annie. She was on her way up and out of Jersey City.

Both she and her mother moved into Manhattan in a fashionable apartment on the Upper West Side. A doorman building that had a concierge also.

She still had childhood girlfriends in Jersey City and every so often she would go back to visit them in the ghetto.

Annie went back once too often.

It is suggested that after each story you _wait_ a moment or so and think about the people you just read about before going on. Thank you.

4 - Atlantic Beach

When Donna didn't call her parents that night they started to worry. She had just moved into her first apartment a few months ago and always called them in the evening. Donna was mentally challenged and had been working full time for years to save enough to move out of the group home and be independent.

They knew something was wrong.

Donnas' parents waited till nine and then drove over to her apartment to see what was going on.

They knew Donna didn't drive and her workplace was only a few blocks from the apartment. Something had to be wrong.

Upon entering they called out her name but there was no response.

They noticed the furniture was askew and there seemed to be blood all over the living room.

As they walked further into the apartment blood was everywhere. Walls, floor, and it trailed into the bathroom. When her father looked in the tub he saw her lifeless body listlessly lying there in a pool of red.

He immediately called the police.

When the detectives finally came they looked around and saw blood splatter all over and knew there had been a terrible struggle. On the floor of the kitchen was a twelve inch knife covered in blood. Carefully they bagged it as this was obviously the murder weapon.

Now they had to find the killer.

There was no appearance of forced entry or rape. So they figured she had to know her killer.

Donna was the oldest child. She had a younger brother and sister. They were the only people she socialized with. Donna did not date. She just went to work and came right home.

The police wanted to question the brother but he was in Iraq serving in the army.

When they questioned where her sister was they found out she lived in town only a few minutes away.

The sister, Deedee, worked as a dancer in a gentleman's club and was a known intravenous drug user. She had been arrested previously on drug and prostitution charges but was never convicted.

When the police went to her house the next day they were told by a neighbor that she left for Florida with her boyfriend.

Meanwhile the police lab did tests on the knife and found a bloody fingerprint on it that matched the sister's. So an arrest warrant was issued and the Florida state police were notified that she might be there.

Deedee had worked in a club in Orland before and also had an arrest record there for burglary and drug possession.

All things pointed to her.

About two weeks later she was captured in Florida and extradited back to New Jersey.

When Deedee was born her sister was sixteen and her older brother was twelve. Donna loved her little sister and was taught by her parents to help out and watch over her little sister. She took this literally and her whole life did what she could for her.

But at the trial it came out that Deedee had gone to Donna for money for drugs. She gave it to her every time except for this instance. This led to a drug induced rage and Deedee killed her sister and broke her neck in the struggle.

The prosecutor introduced evidence at trial that only two people were aware of.

When Donna was sixteen and in an institution she was raped and got pregnant. Donna never understood, or questioned anything. Her parents kept the rape a secret.

Deedee was raised as her sister.

It is suggested that after each story you *wait* a moment or so and think about the people you just read about before going on. Thank you.

5 – The Rabbi

The Rabbi would never eat pork. It was not kosher and it was forbidden for him to eat.

In his whole life he had never even touched anything from a pig, let alone eat it.

He was a young rabbi in his late thirties and was single. He had studied in Israel as well as the rabbinical colleges in America.

Now he was hired for a new synagogue with a mostly young congregation. It was his first congregation and he really wanted to do well.

The older women in the congregation started to talk to him about their nieces and granddaughters. A marriage with the rabbi wouldn't be so bad. Actually they thought it would be great as he was young, educated and had a wholesome look about him.

He wasn't a bad-looking fellow. Kind of thin, wore glasses, and was very friendly and soft-spoken.

On Tuesdays, his day off, he would go to the bookstore to see what new books had come in. As was his custom, he would buy a book, walk to the coffee shop in the bookstore, and read while sipping his coffee.

Then one day a young woman came into the crowded coffee shop and asked if he would mind if she sat down at his small table as there were no other empty seats available.

Her eyes were light blue and they glowed against her dark brown hair. They call this combination an "American beauty." They were riveting when you looked into them. They were almost like the blue steely eyes of a forest wolf staring at you down his muzzle. It was very hypnotizing.

The rabbi said it was alright to sit with him. There was plenty of space at his table.

Her perfume wafted through the coffee aroma and swept toward the rabbi's face. He smelled her before he saw her.

Then he looked up and looked right into her face.

The most beautiful face he had ever seen. Only God could make a face like this, he thought to himself.

In the earliest days of creation in order for the species to continue they had to mate. To help things along hormones came into play. Thousands of years later they still exist and are for the most part uncontrollable.

It doesn't matter what your upbringing, or how you were raised. When a boy's eyes meet the right girl's eyes, their hormones begin to do what they were meant to do.

When the rabbi looked in the eyes of this most beautiful of women his hormones started to act up. How could he speak to her and not act foolish? He spoke to his congregation every Saturday and was not tongue tied like he was now. What is happening?

The young woman sat down and crossed her legs, with her red plaid skirt settling just above her knees. The gold cross she was wearing was glistening as were her red polished shoes that matched the color of her fingernails. So perfect, so put together.

"Hi," she said, introducing herself. "Do you come here often?" she asked.

The rabbi's mind started to race. She is not Jewish, she probably eats pork products. What if we start talking and find out we like each other? She is so beautiful. What if something develops and we go out on a date.

Is it okay to kiss non-kosher lips? What a predicament he was in.

Maybe they could meet next Tuesday also, he thought. But he never ushered the words.

It was not to be.

It is suggested that after each story you *wait* a moment or so and think about the people you just read about before going on. Thank you.

6 - Selma

I marched in Selma. The civil rights battle was my battle also. The Klu Klux Klan didn't distinguish between Jews and blacks. We were the same to them.

The rights of black Americans were my rights also.

I felt I had to march in unison with them. I left college for a semester to go south on the freedom buses with some other people who felt the same as I did.

I sat next to a black girl named Daisy who lived in Brooklyn. We got on the same bus by coincidence as hundreds of people from the tristate area all came to the Greyhound bus station to go south for the march.

Daisy was cool and we spoke about many subjects. Her skin was not that dark, a caramel color, and she wore her hair in a white style with a curl just above the shoulders. Her eyes were dark brown and they contrasted against her skin tone very nicely. She was wearing jeans and a baggy plaid shirt. She had thin lips and a wider nose. I thought she was very pretty. I didn't see her color after a while. She just became a girl who was sitting next to me on the bus. And I was interested in her.

It was a long bus ride and we stopped in Baltimore where we were able to grab something to eat. I bought her lunch as we had become good friends on the bus, and I liked her.

She was a singer in a supper club in Harlem on the weekends and she worked in a store during the day selling clothing on 125th street. Her mother had died when she was younger and she lived with her father who was a postman in Greenwich Village.

By the time we reach Alabama we knew everything about each other. Her family history and how they settled in New York. I told her of my grandfather Ben who came from Latvia to escape the pogroms. We had more in common than most people would expect. Her father's family left the South when the Klan tried to kidnap his brother and hang him. So the family left the next day.

My older sister Elli had wavy hair but the Joan Baez look was in, so she used to go to black beauty parlors and have them straighten her hair. The white beauty parlors didn't know how to do it.

Daisy and I were the only ones in our families who were born and raised in New York.

Finally the bus arrived in Montgomery and we got off. The organizers of the march had our names and arranged for buses and vans to take us to different churches to sleep in. Daisy stayed with me and we were driven to a small Baptist church in the city.

We arrived after the first day of the march which was turned back at the Edmund Pettis Bridge.

The second day we were bused to Selma to join in the march to Montgomery. Daisy and I were part of the twenty-five thousand people who marched with Dr. Martin Luther King. We slept in the fields and the sweet smell of the pastures at night stays with me to this day.

Yes, as they say in Hollywood, Daisy and I became very good friends.

I am now teaching in a college near Boston and she sings at night in clubs in the area.

It is over forty years since we rode together.

I married a girl that I met on a bus.

It is suggested that after each story you _wait_ a moment or so and think about the people you just read about before going on. Thank you.

7 - Frankie

Frankie was just arrested and put in the county jail until he either raises one hundred thousand dollars bail or goes to trial. As an addict he did not have any money that was not spent on drugs.

It is now March and they set a trial date for February of next year. So much for a fair and speedy trial.

He was arrested for burglary and possession of a stolen car. He admitted to my daughter, the mother of his son, that he did something stupid and was caught. We found out because there is a phone number you can call in New Jersey and find out what charges a person is being held on. It is public knowledge.

His wife and newborn daughter live in Philadelphia. He rarely came into New Jersey because there was a warrant out for his arrest on some other charges. He came once too often.

A friend of mine once told me that when a person takes heroin, heroin takes the person. In this case it's true.

Frankie is very thin and frail looking and has tattoos all over his arms and neck. He got a lot of them when he did a prison term for the eight burglaries he did a few years earlier with my daughter. That's how he came into my life.

He wasn't as fortunate as my daughter was. We could afford a long-term treatment center that took almost a whole year to clean her up and kept her out of prison.

While my daughter was in a county jail awaiting trial she would call and plead with us to bail her out. But after she stole our car, antiques, and jewelry from us we knew better than to let an addict into our home again.

She stayed there until we were able to get her into a long-term treatment facility. She spent three months in jail where she drew pictures for the other inmates of their children so they could have it tattooed on their arms when they got out.

Frankie was in special education classes when he did go to school. He comes from a dysfunctional family.

He would play hooky for days and hang out with his uncle who was an alcoholic and drug addict. His mother got pregnant when she was fourteen and had Frank's older brother.

Her daughters and granddaughters get all her attention. Not once in ten years has she called her grandson to say hello. How's school? What's up in your life? She is this way with her sons and her grandsons. They don't exist in her world. . I believe she has a dislike for men.

When Frankie was sober and cleaned up my son got him a job in a distribution warehouse. He was doing okay. He was a hard worker. I heard very good reports on his work and attitude.

Then he started with the drugs again.

He couldn't keep clean unless he was in jail.

But to his credit he really loves his son and took great pride in him. Frankie would play with him when my daughter would bring him over to his mother's house. If Frankie wasn't nodding off from drugs he would talk to him and play catch with him.

His was a lost soul and life.

Then we got the phone call from Frankie's mother.

He was killed in a race riot at the county jail because he was white.

It is suggested that after each story you *wait* a moment or so and think about the people you just read about before going on. Thank you.

8 – The Funeral

As the priest entered the funeral home in Brooklyn he was greeted by the extended family members who were also grieving.

The widow was wearing the obligatory black clothes with a veil pushed over her forehead. Sitting next to her were her three children from Sonny, and one from her previous late husband, Gino.

Slowly the priest walked over to her and held her hand and offered his blessing for her and her children. She was a regular at church every day.

She wondered how this could happen a second time. First Gino was taken, then Sonny. It's not fair, she thought to herself.

Yes, they were doing stuff they shouldn't have been doing, but it wasn't that bad that they had to be whacked. She never knew what they exactly did for a living. It had something to do with air conditioning and construction sales for office buildings. That was what they both told her and she had no reason to suspect otherwise.

In the middle of the room was the coffin with Sonny laid out nice and proper in a dark blue suit. It was similar to the suit he always wore to work.

The Fattachie Family Funeral Home was very ornately decorated. A lot of gold and bronze, with burgundy carpets everywhere to be seen. Marble on the floors where there was no carpet.

There were the old rumors that the mob owned the place but it was never proven. Although Sonny's funeral was being paid for by his boss at the construction sales office, no one thought it unusual. It often happened that way. At least Sonny was found and didn't just disappear. There was closure for the family.

When the room started to get crowded, the sobbing widow looked around, then stood up and threw herself against the casket, and started to wail and cry for her Sonny.

Her sisters came over and placed their arms around her. The flabby skin under their arms waved in the air as they tried to pry her from the heavy carved cross on top of the casket. No one in the neighborhood could say she didn't grieve for her husband in a proper fashion.

Yet there was Sonny lying flat, out in the open casket, with the bright white polyester lining contrasting against his blue suit.

The men who came to pay their respects had the usual nicknames one finds in this area of Brooklyn.

Many of them were nicknamed after body parts. Three Fingers, the Lip, the Nose, and other similar monikers.

They were mostly large men with pock-marked or scarred faces. They were street guys. They all grew up knowing one another or were friends with people who knew them and made the "introductions."

They all came over individually to the widow once she sat down again and offered their most sincere condolences.

One Toe Tony was there also. Nobody spoke to him. They didn't even acknowledge he was there. He was a bigger than life guy who you never missed when he entered a room. He was loud and outgoing with a smile that could warm the devil's heart. But you didn't want to mess with him. He had a very quick temper and was extremely violent. He was the boss' right hand man.

One Toe Tony didn't say a word this evening. He was as quiet as a church mouse.

That was because he was lying in a false bottom just beneath Sonny.

It is suggested that after each story you *wait* a moment or so and think about the people you just read about before going on. Thank you.

9 - Patsy

Patsy had a small shop on the avenue. It was his first business and he was doing okay with it.

Everyone had bugs, or mice, or rats in New York City. He decided not to go into the family construction business and he opened a pest control and exterminating company in Brooklyn.

The toughest part was getting people to work for him. He paid them well but you have to go into dark, dank apartment basements that were ridden with fleas and other pests and spray or bomb them. It was not for the squeamish or faint of heart.

Patsy also did restaurants because the New York City Board of Health mandated that they get a certificate from an exterminator on a monthly basis. Depending on how much they wanted to pay (usually not a lot), Patsy would either use the strong chemicals or dilute them with water if the job was to be done on the cheap.

He had a picture hanging in his office of a job he did for a restaurant on one of the beaches on Long Island. He was standing behind a huge pile of large dead rats almost three feet high that he had poisoned the night before.

The store he rented was very small and consisted of himself and a secretary who would take the calls. She would also do the books and very often he would do her.

Although he was married with kids and lived on Long Island in a very nice area he liked to play around with the girls from Brooklyn. Especially if the girls were well endowed.

After his father died his mother took over the family meetings in her house and the uncles would come when she wanted to have a sit-down and discuss "things."

She called Patsy one afternoon that she wanted him to come for dinner after work because she had something to talk to him about. But Patsy had a date that night with a local blond with big boobs. So he didn't go after work to see his mother.

The next day a man walked into the doorway of his store and stood there. He was so big that his shoulders didn't fit between the door frames unless he turned sideways.

"Patsy, you mudder wantz ta know why youse didn't come see her afder work yes-derday," he said with his deep Brooklyn accent.

He couldn't believe it. His own mother sent someone for him. Dammit, he thought. Now he's in the doghouse with her.

But a mother always forgives her son, after a little anguish of course.

The business grew over the years.

He once bought another business to get the workers. Soon after the sale, half the new accounts dropped the service. They were the seller's friends and relatives.

Patsy said he wasn't paying any more on the purchase. He was threatened when two men walked into his shop and demanded the money owed. So Patsy called his uncle.

He was to meet his uncle in the back booth of a restaurant in Red Hook. The uncle said he was going to kill the guy, his family, his mother and all his relatives. Patsy said he just wanted to not pay, not kill anyone.

The next day Patsy got a call that it was all a misunderstanding. Forget the money owed.

He usually got a $10,000 check each month from a union for work he did for different buildings. Sometimes he didn't even have to do anything.

He started to buy real estate, other "investments" and eventually bought a building to expand his business into.

Free enterprise works in America.

It is suggested that after each story you _wait_ a moment or so and think about the people you just read about before going on. Thank you.

10 - Bernard

Bernard was a flaming gay. He lived in squalor in San Francisco in the Heights with his other addict buddies.

He was usually strung out and high. His tall, thin frame barely had the strength to hold him up. His thick black-rimmed glasses would often slip from the bridge of his nose when he stood up. There was nothing there to hold them up. He was HIV positive with full blown AIDS.

His friends often called him Bernice due to the women's clothing he liked to wear when he was working the streets.

He wasn't a nice person. He had a mean streak in him and would say and do vengeful things that hurt many people. But he didn't care.

But now he didn't work so much. He didn't have the strength.

Only when he needed a fix did he push himself to go out and party. It was too late for him and he knew it.

He had led a life of addiction and unprotected homosexual sex and now he was paying for it.

The blouse he had on was extremely loose and the bra was stuffed with tissues. He couldn't afford the operation for the implants that he desired due to his heroin habit.

But life wasn't always this way for him.

He was an accountant by trade and had a wife somewhere on the East Coast. She had moved after the divorce and he lost track of her when he moved to California.

He was never handsome or even considered good looking. He was gangly with a big nose. But he had a change of life moment when he found out he was attracted to men. That ended his marriage. His children never heard or saw him again either.

It was now evening and the dark shadows under his eyes were hidden by the makeup he put on. The lipstick was slightly smeared and he gave up trying to put on mascara due to his hands shaking.

He slid on his panties, put on flats, grabbed a purse and started down the stairs.

The bus took him to his favorite corner where gay men went to pick up a date for the evening. He was a known figure there and not many men spoke to him because they knew he had medical issues. Only the newbie's who drove in from out of town would stop to pick him up.

This night a dark van stopped. Bernice had a conversation with the driver, and he got in. They had a little small talk while they drove to a secluded alley behind some buildings.

There was nobody in the alley except for the van. Then two young men from the backseat jumped out of the van, pulled Bernice from the passenger seat, and started to beat him.

They had baseball bats and an iron pipe. They spat on him while they mercilessly beat him and yelled out obscene curses.

Finally when the men exhausted themselves, they all got back in the van. They backed the van up and drove over the listless body lying there in the alley.

Then they drove away.

They were laughing and said they wanted to do it again to another fag.

Bernie wasn't a nice person. He had a mean streak in him and would say and do vengeful things that hurt many people. And he didn't care.

And neither did his attackers.

It is suggested that after each story you *wait* a moment or so and think about the people you just read about before going on. Thank you.

11 - The Bakery

It was a small bakery off the Grand Concourse in the Bronx. Freshly made cakes, rolls, and pastries were sold there.

Part-time college students were always hired as they had varied class schedules and were available to work the long odd hours needed.

One of the college girls at the Italian bakery was Judy. She was a chubby girl with a huge buxom, very outgoing, and was an asset to the bakery sales staff. Her long black hair was tied back into a ponytail and covered with a head net when she worked. She always wore black leather from head to toe.

She was also having a rough time of things personally. She felt that no one really would love her, due to her weight, so she was promiscuous with a lot of men. But Judy did practice safe sex and insisted that her dates use condoms. She carried them in her pocketbook at all times.

Once she teamed up with another girl at the shop after work and joined in a threesome for the other girl's boyfriend's birthday. This was sort of a gift to him from his girlfriend.

They took the bus to his apartment and they all undressed and went at it as soon as they closed the front door.

Judy did not discriminate on the age of the fellows she dated. Some were her age, some a little older, and some were old enough to be her grandfather.

She had an affair with one of the bakers at the shop. He would take her out to practice driving in his car after work once she got her permit. Then they would park and she would thank him with her favors. It was the least she could do to say thanks.

Depression was only thinly veiled below the surface. She was the youngest of six children and the only girl. Her father was a detective in a local Bronx precinct and was always taking his family on expensive vacations.

The other police officers, who lived in the area but not in his precinct, were always struggling to pay their bills and make ends meet. But not Judy's father.

He liked to tend to his garden and was always in the backyard digging and planting. It was a mini botanical garden back there. He said it relaxed him.

Then there were the Special Commission hearings on police corruption and many officers were brought up on charges. Drug money, cash, was flowing into the police precincts like an open faucet.

Judy's father was caught up in it and forced to resign but not before he made a deal with the prosecutor.

To get a non-prison sentence he agreed to cooperate. He turned the state's evidence on many of his brother officers.

The family got death threats constantly and was in fear for their lives.

Finally it died down and over the years the family kind of resumed a somewhat normal life. They always looked over their shoulders when they went out. Many men went to jail because of his testimony and had their lives ruined.

Judy's father got away with just losing his job and reputation.

But he was able to continue with his lavish lifestyle in spite of this.

Interestingly he still puttered around his garden. No new shrubs or bushes were put in.

He just continued digging and replanting the same bushes all the time.

And he kept on smiling.

It is suggested that after each story you *wait* a moment or so and think about the people you just read about before going on. Thank you.

12 - Keisha

She was tall, about five feet ten inches with long black hair, and usually wore an above the knees skirt showing plenty of leg.

Her black skin was not dark, but not light either. She had some tattoos on her arms with the names and pictures of her two children. She was only twenty-seven and a single parent. She never married the two men who fathered her children, nor thought she had to. There was no need to, although she would have liked it. They were office affairs and she said many times they would not last. And they didn't. Keisha was very independent.

But Keisha had a quick temper and when something bothered her she exploded. That's why the men in her life don't hang around long. Just enough to get some booty and then they are gone.

She had her first child when she was only sixteen. It happened on the roof of the project she lived in with her mother. Her first boyfriend was twenty-two at the time, worked in the bodega with her, and she was fifteen when they went up there on a warm summer evening.

There was a small rooftop garden that the community had planted and they had left some beach chairs to sit and enjoy the light breeze that blew in.

They were twelve stories up and the view was pleasant, though it was a cityscape.

Sitting up there he put his arm around her, they kissed, and then they spread out a blanket and lay down together. It was approaching midnight and no one was up there except the two of them. That's how she became pregnant the first time.

After the first child was born, she agreed to raise the child until it was thirteen, then it would have to live with the father until emancipation at eighteen. That's how it went down.

About eight years later she became pregnant with another co-worker's child and they were going to move in together. He was a dirt bag and a weasel. Thin, sneaky, had small beady eyes and he shuffled from job to job and was not a stable person. No one knows if she had an abortion or a miscarriage but the living arrangement fell through, and she wasn't pregnant anymore.

The third pregnancy happened again with a co-worker. They were going to get engaged when she became pregnant. They did move in together and everything seemed to be going great. The baby came and there was only happiness.

But one day when the baby was about eight months old her temper flared up over a stupid argument and she attacked her fiancé. He defended himself and the police were called. He didn't want to go to jail so he decided to move out and not live with her anymore.

She now had a good job with a big chain retailer and was promoted to assistant manager. She had no time for the baby so her ex-fiancé took care of his child and had the baby move in with him. He paid her rent and child care until he took the baby full time. Then she was on her own again.

On weekends, every now and then, she would take him for a Saturday or Sunday.

She was single again, in her mind, and was back on the dating scene.

No kids, no complications, money to spend on herself, no one to report to and free as a bird.

At twenty-seven she was fifteen again.

It is suggested that after each story you <u>wait</u> a moment or so and think about the people you just read about before going on. Thank you.

13 - Bart

His parents were holocaust survivors and after the war they settled in England before they immigrated to the United States.

They came to Brooklyn because they had relatives who came before the war.

It was a nice neighborhood near Brooklyn College. Tree-lined streets, good schools, peaceful and quiet, and it was a wonderful place to raise a family.

One son, Bart, was born to them and he was very athletic. But he had an arrogant personality. He was not honest and had an aggressive attitude about him. He was just the opposite of his parents.

During the summer of 1962 the son came into good fortune.

One day he invited all his friends into his basement to see his new train set. It was fantastic. It had miniature trees, buildings, cars, people, a full set of trains and track all laid out on a four-by-eight plywood board. It had to be worth over a thousand dollars. His family did not live that way and it was very unusual for them to spend that amount on hobby trains.

The parents lived modestly, drove a compact Plymouth, and were not flashy people.

No one could figure out how he got all that train equipment.

About a week later one of his neighborhood friends were going to the train station and noticed the glass door to the hobby shop was broken. All the guys went there to buy toys and stuff to play with. The owner was an older man who was very upset over a break-in that happened the week before. Expensive trains and other hobby stuff that would go with them were stolen. He didn't have insurance as it was a very "good neighborhood" and no one had burglar alarms in 1962 except jewelry stores.

What a coincidence the friend thought.

Then after high school he went to the local college. After graduation he decided to become a medical doctor. He was accepted into a school in Mexico.

Time went by and eventually he set up a practice in Harlem catering to Medicare patients. He drove a Mercedes, wore expensive clothes, and lived the high lifestyle his parents never enjoyed nor wanted.

It turned out he had a Medicare mill.

Congress soon began an investigation. He was named in the newspapers as a Medicare mill doctor who sent patients for tests they did not need in order to build up his bill. A Senator went undercover and was "treated" by Dr. Bart in his medical office.

The *New York Daily News* and all the other newspapers, including the *New York Times*, carried the story.

Eventually it went away.

Either he had good lawyers who saw to it that matters were taken care of or the prosecutors were inept. To this day no one knows how it went down except he kept his medical license.

He married one of his patients who was a much younger black woman, who was well endowed, and they lived on the Upper West Side of Manhattan.

Today he has a very large practice where he hires newly licensed doctors to practice medicine in his office. They spend less than five minutes with a patient and bill Medicare and Medicaid huge fees for their time and tests.

After forty years nothing has changed.

It is suggested that after each story you <u>wait</u> a moment or so and think about the people you just read about before going on. Thank you.

14 - The Bar

She slowly stalked a spot at the bar. Quietly she was walking between crowded bodies waiting for a seat.

The stool next to the young man in the suit was her prey.

It was not just a seat, but a seat next to a fashionably dressed yuppie that smelled great, and of money.

He was a trader with a Wall Street brokerage firm. He stopped in after the market closed about once a week or so to get a drink and meet other traders to talk about the Yankees. Who had the better box seats in the stadium? Were they going to the Giants games next season?

It didn't hurt if they met an attractive person there. It was known as a hot spot to meet and greet wealthy traders and the men and women who worked in Wall Street knew it.

Soon the seat next to him opened up and she slid onto it without a moment's hesitation.

A conversation was started between them and with laughter, smiles, and a few quick-witted quips a new friendship was evolving.

He had goals in his life. He wanted a new Mercedes every two years, a bigger summer house in the Hamptons, a few Rolexes, more money in his 401K, and enough tax free bonds to carry him for the rest of his life. His net worth today was only a few million but he was on his way to a hundred million, given a handful of years.

Not surprisingly those were her goals also. But she wasn't going to get there by working on Wall Street. She was going to work Wall Street until she made a big killing by marrying someone there.

Her short blonde hair contrasted against her deep green suit with the ultra-short skirt that stopped just short of heaven. She called it that because the men she had bedded on her quest were in heaven once they reached it.

The gym workout every day for two hours didn't go to waste. It was an investment in her future. Some people went to college to get ahead in life but she invested in her body. That was her vehicle for success.

She was registered with a top modeling agency and it was not unusual to see her on fashion spreads in *Vogue* and other high style publications.

In her past was the banker she almost hooked. He worked for a big international bank and was always traveling on business. He would be in Asia this week and Europe the next.

Sometimes he was gone for almost a month but she didn't care. He had set her up in a Park Avenue apartment and she was living the good life. Everything she wanted was taken care of by his personal assistant.

Everything....

But all good things come to an end and when it was over, she had to start looking for a new suitor.

This one in the bar was looking good.

He had a great smile, white teeth, and was fascinated with her.

The Venus flytrap was about to spring shut. The fly smelled the nectar from her as it softly floated upwards. It was about to land on the lip of the petal.

Its wings were fluttering and the tasty morsel was about to be eaten when the fly changed course.

The young man looked into the bar mirror, excused himself, and turned to the fellow who just walked in right behind him.

"I was waiting for you," he said. Then they kissed and walked out together.

It is suggested that after each story you _wait_ a moment or so and think about the people you just read about before going on. Thank you.

15 - Carl

Carl was eighteen and couldn't get laid in a brothel holding hundred dollar bills in his hand. That was the kind of luck Carl had.

He was a good-looking young man with chiseled facial features, a full head of hair, and an outgoing personality. He thought of male modeling but he never really pursued it.

Carl wore casual clothes that everyone wore in Brooklyn College. Nothing fancy yet it was practical.

As a freshman in college he had a summer job selling ice cream on the beach at Reis Park in Far Rockaway.

He didn't have to work hard. Many days he didn't even have to work. Other men would pay him to sell his ice cream for him. It seems he was assigned to the nude beach at the park and he didn't have to take off his clothes to work there.

Then in the spring, he met this young girl at a club in Manhattan one Saturday night and they hit it off and exchanged phone numbers.

On Monday he called her and they spoke every night that week. She lived in Connecticut and she invited him up for the day. So on Saturday he took off from work and went up there to visit.

He was wearing his grandfather's wool hound's-tooth trench coat and he had a little trouble finding the address. Seems it was a horse farm in the countryside with white picket fences. Very Waspish and old money he thought.

The girl was your typical blonde girl from the suburbs. She was very friendly but not worldly at all. Carl was introduced to her parents who looked at him as if he was from another planet.

Her mother said that two young men she knew from the area were coming over to see her.

Carl said that when the two fellows could have been named Biff and Chad. Needless to say the date was a disaster.

But Carl didn't give up. He met another young girl one night and they drove in his car to the end of Bay Parkway in the old Korvette's parking lot.

It was deserted at two in the morning. There was only a few tall parking lights lit and he tried to park in the middle of the lot where it was darker.

He was making progress. They started to kiss and he was able to unhook her bra. This had the makings of a successful evening. He already reached second base and was heading for third.

The windows were starting to fog up and he was excited about what was about to happen.

As was his luck, just then a car full of Chinese teenage boys drove onto the lot. They saw his car and what was going on. They began to drive in circles around his car blowing their horn and yelling out the window in Chinese at them. They were laughing and having a great time spoiling Carl's great time.

Needless to say, the girl's mood quickly changed and Carl's little party was over. He drove her home and never saw her again.

It was this way for years. He met them, dated them, kissed them, but never got lucky with them.

And then he bought a car. Carl wanted a classic old car.

So he bought a ten year old Datsun, without asking anyone's advice, with the floor boards rotted out. If you sat in the passenger seat you could actually see the road below.

Once on the Marine Parkway Bridge the front wheel came off while he was driving.

Even with cars he had no luck.

It is suggested that after each story you *wait* a moment or so and think about the people you just read about before going on. Thank you.

16 - Abby

Abby had a great singing voice and her flowing black hair swayed when she moved at the microphone. The auditorium was at capacity to hear this young girl from the local high school.

It started at home. She would hear the radio that her mother kept on while cleaning the house. Soon she started to remember the words and melodies. As she got older she improvised so she had a tone that was all her own.

One day she tried out for her school choir and the teacher was floored when "that voice" came out of that small body. Soon Abby was singing the lead in front of the choir and the school concerts were beginning to sell out.

One day she was heard by a talent agent and was signed to a contract with Sony Records.

Number one hits started to roll in, concert tours, national recognition, and more money than she knew what to do with.

Abby had to hire an agent, a business manager, an accounting firm, a law firm, a personal hairstylist, a wardrobe lady, and even a personal assistant. She was working and working and getting tired.

One of her posse offered her some pills to help get her up for the next performance. Then she had to take some pills to get down so she could sleep. The hours on the road were terrible and a strain on her.

She had just finished a performance in Pigeon Ford Tennessee when she left and rented a car and just took off. She abandoned the tour, the posse, and everything.

Driving down the back highway that ran parallel to the interstate highway, she saw a local church sitting in the field. She pulled off the road and drove up to the small one-room church that was in the middle of a field.

She walked in the church and sat down. Abby was exhausted. But then a feeling came over her. Almost like there was a spirit sitting next to her, and she felt calm and relaxed.

Then she heard her grandmother's voice praying next to her, just like when she was a little girl in church.

Services weren't until next Sunday and there was nobody around that she could see. She sat for an hour and many thoughts ran through her mind.

Was all the fame worth it? She started to look inward at herself and felt there was more to life than what she was doing.

She needed to commit herself to something that would make her life meaningful.

Although she was raised in a church-going family, she had drifted away from her faith through the years. Never abandoning it, Abby just placed faith on the sideline of her life.

Was this a message? Did she really hear what she thought she heard?

She looked around but saw no one. Yet she heard her grandmother pray to Jesus right here in this small church.

The reverend entered the church and sat down next to her. He welcomed her and hoped she found what she was looking for.

They started to talk.

He explained that her singing had brought a lot of comfort to the sick and hopeless in his congregation and he wanted to say thank you. He never expected her to be in his church with him.

Perplexed, confused, yet relaxed, she thanked him and got in her car and drove away.

She felt at peace with herself. She stopped the car at the end of the driveway and looked back.

But there was no church. It was gone.

It is suggested that after each story you _wait_ a moment or so and think about the people you just read about before going on. Thank you.

17 – Tar Beach

Tar beach was Belinda's favorite place to sun herself. Carefully she laid out the oversized beach blanket and started to undress.

She was thirty stories up on a high rise in the middle of Manhattan.

The only people who would be able to see her were in another high-rise building one block away. And they would have to use a telescope to even make out who she was.

Feeling comfortable she took off her clothes and placed them neatly in a pile on a corner of the blanket.

Her lightly colored skin glistened in the sun with sweat. The temperature was over ninety degrees today and she started to put on her coconut tanning lotion.

Slowly her hands glided over her torso, gently swirling the lotion to cover all of her.

Belinda laid down, closed her eyes, and started to think of things, especially about her ex-boyfriend. She had just broken up with him and it was a bad breakup.

Her parents didn't like him because they thought he was controlling and would not amount to anything.

They were very religious people and worked hard to attain the American dream.

Her father went to college in the sixties at City College. At that time there were very few African Americans getting a higher education. But he was determined to succeed and make a better life for himself.

Belinda herself had graduated college. She was an English major and wanted to be a reporter for a newspaper. But the city papers weren't hiring. In fact they were all downsizing and her counselor at school suggested she try for an internship with a television station. That's where she met her boyfriend.

It didn't matter that he was married.

They would go for lunch, have a drink or two, kid around with each other then they would go back to his office to "relax."

This went on for months.

He promised her a permanent position at the station in the newsroom. Belinda would be writing copy for the early morning telecast and sitting in the six AM news pod with the other girls.

Her boyfriend was an executive at the station and he was very domineering. He took advantage of her in many ways and she was so in love with him she took his verbal abuse willingly.

Years before she was diagnosed as a schizophrenic with bipolar disease. The medications she was on sometimes worked and sometimes didn't.

When they stopped working she would get depressed and even violent towards people she loved. She couldn't help herself.

It was working now but there were no guarantees it would continue. She had been on many drugs before this one, but her body eventually adjusted to them and would stop working.

Stress also didn't help.

She was under a psychologist's care and would see her once a week. She used to see her two or three times a week but she had been improving.

All was peaceful on the roof.

She had brought along a small radio and was listening to music and trying to get the thoughts of her ex out of her mind. But they just kept popping up and she couldn't control her thoughts. She was getting depressed thinking about him.

Finally she realized she couldn't unwind. She was now very agitated.

Belinda stood up and slowly walked to the edge of the roof.

Thirty stories high, she just looked down. Completely naked, the high winds buffeted her as she stood there. Goosebumps popped up on her skin.

She decided she had to leave the beach….

It is suggested that after each story you *wait* a moment or so and think about the people you just read about before going on. Thank you.

18 - Casino

I don't remember the exact year but I know it was when I was in high school. Probably this took place in the early sixties.

My friends and I played cards, poker to be exact, and we only used chips to bet with. None of us had any real money.

My uncle had a furniture store and although I was still a teenager, I used to work on the delivery truck on Saturdays.

He paid me a few dollars, not much really, but the tips were good. It wasn't unusual for me to make over thirty dollars on a good day. But I worked my rear end off lugging the furniture into people's homes.

So one day with the money I had earned I decided that if my friends liked to gamble, why not help them do it?

My parents had a big old Victorian house in the Midwood section (Ditmas Park) of Brooklyn with an attic that was empty. They never went up there except for storage of suitcases

When it was built just before the 1920s, it had a maid's apartment up there with a full bathroom and two bedrooms.

Since it wasn't being used, I thought, why not put it to use? So I bought a small toy roulette table, an electric vibrating horse-racing track, and set up my mother's folding bridge table.

My sister had a small math toy that if you pushed the handle down, it had three wheels with a number on each wheel that would turn, and a math problem would appear in the windows. I improvised and put colored paper squares over the numbers and thereby built my own slot machine.

Steve Wynn had nothing on me then. I was ahead of my time.

I hired two of my friends and told them they would get a cut of the profits.

I had one room set up for gambling. It was on the small side but I was able to fit everything in and figured I could hold plenty of guys because no one was sitting.

Then I realized I needed entertainment.

Somebody to kind of loosen up the party so everyone would feel like gambling.

I wasn't eighteen yet and neither were my friends so alcohol was out. Thinking out loud the solution came to me. The casino needed a showgirl to schmooze with the guys.

There was this girl in school that everyone knew. She was a grade ahead of me. Her name was Deena. She had white/pink-streaked hair and was also known as Deenis the Penis for obvious reasons. Remember that this was probably 1962 or so.

Anyway Deena agreed to "work the room" for me and she was allocated the other bedroom in the attic for her schmoozing.

I never saw what went on in there but I had a good idea.

Opening day got off to a great start.

Word was spread throughout the high school and you had to buy a ticket to be admitted to my house. I figured this was just another income stream.

The first day was a hit.

My employees made a bundle, Deena also did very well, and I was sure I was onto a new career after high school.

The second day started off even better with a lot more guys coming in. Then the Feds, in the guise of my mother, decided to walk upstairs and see why thirty teenage boys were in her attic.

Although I wasn't sent to Attica, I was sentenced to solitary confinement in my room for a month after school.

It is suggested that after each story you *wait* a moment or so and think about the people you just read about before going on. Thank you.

19 – Summer at Blue Meadow Lake

She was standing there laughing when we crashed the party. Blue Meadow Lake had a large Jewish population, considering it was in the middle of nowhere, and we were looking for girls. If they were Jewish it just made it better for us.

Teenagers are only interested in one thing. And it doesn't matter what their religion, color, or political thoughts are.

Leslie was a tall girl, thin with long, wispy, blonde hair. She looked like a gentile girl and not a Jewish one. I was very attracted to her.

During the day she was a camp counselor at a hotel nearby.

So I asked her out.

We went out a few times but it didn't go anywhere. She was fun to be with but I couldn't even get a kiss goodnight.

One night we were all in the car and we drove with the girls onto the beach. There were eight of us in a big 1958 Pontiac.

Unfortunately there was also a cop in an unmarked car parked at the beach. He made everyone get out and had the girls walk home. Then he escorted us out of town and warned us not to come back.

This reminded me of a fellow I was introduced to a few years ago who was a real sleaze. He was to go on a first date with this girl and when she opened the door he entered and they started to talk.

He told her he felt there was a sexual tension between them so why not just have sex now and then they can go out and be all relaxed. Needless to say the date ended very quickly.

Lake Hopatcong in northwest New Jersey was a great place to meet girls in the early sixties. It had been a hot spot for years with the Bon Air Lodge bringing in singles from the city. This was before Fire Island and the Hamptons were a magnet for Manhattanites.

Then one night my friends and I were driving along the main road in Landing and we waved at some girls walking along the road. We just yelled out and then continued along.

That night we were at a pizza place in town and some guys said that one of the girl's fathers was looking for us. So we told them to call him.

He came tearing into the parking lot with the police right behind them.

"These are the guys," he said to the police. He addressed them by name. Seems he was an auxiliary cop on the force. We asked what we did and the police said we attacked his daughter. We denied it because we didn't do anything. So we ended up in the Rockaway Township police station at midnight.

Our parents were called and they came down to see what this was all about.

It was now one in the morning. My mother asked the father of the girl what his daughter told him. He said he hasn't spoken to her yet. She was out. Some boys had told him we attacked his daughter.

My mother then said, "You mean to tell me that a sixteen-year-old girl is out at one in the morning, you have no idea where she is, or even spoken to her, and you accuse these boys of attacking her?"

In total disgust my mother told the police to either arrest us or we are leaving.

Don't mess with Mom.

This was now the second town we were not wanted in. All in one summer!

We were on a roll.

It is suggested that after each story you *wait* a moment or so and think about the people you just read about before going on. Thank you.

20 - Moses

After forty years of wandering in the desert the People of Israel were on the precipice of entering the Promised Land.

They were tired of schlepping around and going nowhere. So they gathered together one day and pleaded with Heaven. "Please speak to Moses. We have been traipsing through the desert for forty years. It's very hot, the scenery is nothing to speak of, and the sand gets between our toes and is irritating to our skin."

"We know that you can do this for us. You are the only one in heaven and there are no others. And we have always kept you in the forefront of our minds and in our hearts. Plus we have written this pledge on the entrance to every one of our tents."

"If you could see it in your heart to take pity on us and speak to Moses we pledge to tell our children of your miracles, and they their children."

Heaven then sent an angel to speak to Moses. The angel found him sitting on a ledge overlooking the valley below that was in the Promised Land.

"Moishe, Vas Mackster? [What's up] the angel asked in Yiddish.

"Vouse es doose" [what is this?] Moses replied. "I don't know how but we are speaking in a strange language that I never learned" said Moses.

The angel told him that Heaven wanted him to see the future. That would be one of the hundreds of languages his chosen people will speak.

They will be scattered all over the Earth teaching his commandments and trying to make the world a better place to live.

Moses looked out at the great expanse and then saw Mom-a-lers making kreplach, sweet and sour stuffed cabbage, and also potato knishes.

He saw young Hebrew children reading Torah and studying Heaven's laws. But Moses was not satisfied.

"Listen" he said to the angel, "I have so much more to teach them. Let me take one more meander in the desert."

"During the forty years I led them, I wore out 613 pairs of sandals. With each sandal I would instruct the people in another commandment[1]."

---

[1] In the Jewish faith there are 613 commandments that an observant person is to do every day. It covers from the time they wake up till they go to sleep.

"Moses" the angel replied, "we must leave the rest for the future to figure out. You have given them the basis of Heaven's laws, now the people will have to use their brains to finish the job".

The angel said that if Moses could buy a new pair of sandals he could go out one more time.

Moses then went to the tent of Itzick Bloomingdale, the clothier, to buy a new pair of sandals. But he was sold out.

The same thing happened when he went to see Sollie Lauren and his camel etched sandals.

With a deep breath he had no choice but to spend a lot to get a new pair of sandals. He had to go to the designer tent of Manny Manulo Levi. But alas, he too was sold out. But he did have a thick blue fabric for a new pair of pants.

So the angel made a face saving deal with Moses because Heaven favored Moses.

If Moses would instruct the People of Israel to pray every morning and evening, that there was only One in heaven and there were no others, Heaven would allow them into the Promised Land and stop the drifting around. As a bonus heaven would make it rain in the proper season, they will be fruitful, and multiply like the stars in sky.

So Moses did as he was asked and the People of Israel entered the Promised Land.

It is suggested that after each story you *wait* a moment or so and think about the people you just read about before going on. Thank you.

21 – The Back Window

The back window slowly opened without a creak. New windows do that with ease because they are built to slide easily.

Carefully he placed his arms in first and looked around. Then he hoisted the rest of himself through the window and into the back room of the house. He had done this dozens of times before in other neighborhoods and this house was ripe for the pickings.

It was in the middle of the day and no one answered the phone or the doorbell. There was no car parked outside either and no alarm box on the side of the roof.

Unfortunately if it was a larger development that the house was in, where homes were spaced very far apart, he would just kick in the rear door.

He had met some men when he was in state prison that used to come with crow bars and just remove the whole door frame. They said it was easier than kicking in the door. This way they could see the alarm wires and carefully lay the door down flat. The alarm never went off when they did it that way.

Chris was a convicted rapist and burglar, and was once arrested for domestic violence but she dropped the charges against police advice.

He navigated around the first floor of the house, spotting a plasma television that he could take on his way out if there was nothing else upstairs. He saw a penny jar in the kitchen and emptied it of its contents. There were a few dollar bills in it and lots of quarters. Probably about ten dollars' worth, just enough for a burger and fries later.

He used the large knife he carried to pry open a door in the kitchen that was locked. But he found nothing there except for some high-end cooking equipment and a bunch of collector knives. Maybe they had some value but there could be better stuff upstairs.

He started to run upstairs as he felt he was in the house way too long, he thought. Bounding upstairs he headed for the master bedroom. It looked like an upper class family lived there and he was sure there was plenty of jewelry in the master bedroom.

He was dressed in a plaid lumberjack-type shirt and torn jeans. His face was heavily pockmarked and he had a large scar running across his upper lip. That was the result of a bar fight he had when he worked as a bouncer in a strip club in New York.

The doors on the bedrooms were solid wood with very ornate carvings on them.

Plush chocolate brown carpet lined the hallway. This house smelled of money.

He reached the end of the hall and opened the door. He was startled to find someone home in bed. He stood there for a second and froze.

She was home sick from work and had parked the car in the garage and not answered the phone or front door. She was very tired and didn't want to speak to anyone.

It was summertime and she wasn't wearing any bedclothes. She sat up in bed and was as startled as he was.

He looked at her bare breasts and started to walk towards her.

Without saying a word she put her hand under her other pillow and took out a forty-five pistol and got off a few shots at him.

He staggered backwards, having been hit in the chest three times, and collapsed onto the hallway carpet.

His big mistake was this was Texas and not New York.

It is suggested that after each story you *wait* a moment or so and think about the people you just read about before going on. Thank you.

22 – A Gift

As a youngster about the age of twelve or so he discovered that he had a rare ability. It was strictly by accident that he found what he would later call a gift.

Raised in the northwest corner of New Jersey in Sussex County, he was walking in the forest when he saw a small bird on the ground. It had fallen out of its nest and broken its wing.

Carefully he took off his jacket so as not to touch the bird, and brought it home to put in a shoebox. His plan was to feed it and help it get better. He didn't have any money to pay a veterinarian and was afraid the doctor would kill it.

Hoping his mother would know what to feed it, he patiently waited for her to get home. She was a single woman raising him herself. Her husband had died in Vietnam in the war and she never remarried. It was a struggle to make ends meet as there were few jobs around for women in the rural area they lived in. But she tried her best and led a moral life.

When she finally got home he showed her the small baby bird and asked what they could do to help it get better.

Realizing she did not have the money to take it to a doctor, she told him the bird was badly injured and probably would not live long.

They put some water in a small jar lid, placed it in the shoebox, and then they went to bed for the night.

He lay in bed and prayed for a miracle so the baby bird would live.

His prayers were heard in heaven and he felt a spirit to speak to him.

The bedroom lit up and the light woke the boy up. He was told that his sincerity to help an innocent creature did not go unnoticed and the spirit was sent to give him a gift.

With a pure heart that is very rare, the spirit said, you are going to receive this gift from heaven. You can only use it to help others in the spirit that it was given to you; otherwise it will disappear.

The next morning he woke up and went to see how his baby bird was doing.

He picked it up in his hands and the bird's wing was healed. He was a bit unsure of what had happened but he decided that maybe he received something that he could help people with.

The next day he walked to a local nursing home and went in to visit his grandmother. She was very old and had pneumonia. She wasn't expected to live past the weekend. He hugged her and sat with her a little while, then he left for a cup of juice that the nurses always gave him.

When he got back his grandmother was feeling much better and was sitting up and talking.

He was very excited about this and ran home to tell his mother.

He realized what the gift was he had received and decided to use it to help others.

For many years he traveled all over helping people recover from illness and disease.

He led an exemplary life of honesty and good works.

Finally it was his time to go.

An angel appeared one night and took him by his hand, and they both left his room.

But for years after this he was reported to have been seen walking in hospitals all over the world helping people get better.

It is suggested that after each story you *wait* a moment or so and think about the people you just read about before going on. Thank you.

23 – Visiting Virginia

I entered the bar and was picking up a food order I called ahead for.

My daughter was away and my wife and I were babysitting for my granddaughter.

But there was a mix-up on the bar's computer so I had to kill some time while they rushed to do my take-out order.

Sitting at the bar was this bleached blonde, her hair straight down towards her shoulders, with very blue eyes and pink lips nursing her drink and watching the plasma television on the wall.

Her yellow cocktail was in a tall glass with salt around the rim and a straw. Slowly she would put her lips to the straw and gently pull the liquor into her mouth. Swishing it from side to side to get all the taste from it.

She was wearing a very bright lime green halter top that was cut very low. Above her left breast was tattooed some kind of Chinese symbol. Her skin was very fair and the blue tattoo jumped out screaming to be looked at.

But this was Virginia in May and it was warm out. It was expected that people would be dressed coolly.

She casually looked up at me and smiled. Slowly her forefinger pointed to the stool next to hers. There was no one sitting there with her so I went over and sat down.

Her name was Dolly. She was a local girl who came there often to socialize and meet new people. Her husband was away on business, she said, and she was lonely.

I ordered a drink from the bar. It was a light beer and the mug was frozen. It tasted great as it went down smoothly.

We talked about her job as a receptionist at a local doctor's office. It was a fairly boring job except when it was quiet and the doctor would ask her to come in the exam room with him. She always did because he was good looking and paid her well. Very well.

She would never make that kind of money elsewhere so she did what she had to and she enjoyed every minute of it also, she said.

We talked a little more and then she placed her hand on my forearm as we were sitting.

As time went on she told me about her first husband who was an electrician and was out on a job doing an installation of a ceiling fan in a lady's home.

The woman asked him if he wanted a cold drink and one thing led to another. Before long they were in bed having sex. She was very wealthy, very sexy, and the upshot was he left Dolly for this woman.

So Dolly went on a binge and started looking for men to marry her. She finally met one who would take care of her but he traveled a lot. She knew he had needs and in his travels he would take care of them. Most men do, she told me.

I could sense where this was going. Her breasts were small but perky and I would place her in her late twenties.

Dolly only lived a few minutes away and she asked if I would like to come see her house.

Of course I was flattered. I was now in my mid-sixties and felt good that this young girl would even consider having an affair with me.

Just then my food came out and was placed in front of me at the bar.

I told Dolly maybe some other time, wished her well, and left.

It is suggested that after each story you _wait_ a moment or so and think about the people you just read about before going on. Thank you.

24 – Gypsy Girl

The gypsy parked his car in front of the storefront where his family lived. They always lived in a storefront somewhere. They had more room and it was cheaper.

Also they never paid the full rent and skipped out when the need arrived.

Hudson County was the perfect place to settle in. There were plenty of small cities in the county and they could move from city to city to avoid lawsuits when their workmanship was not up to par.

The gypsies that lived in Bayonne knew better than to start where they lived so they preyed on the other cities in Hudson County.

Only once did they ever cause a problem there. It was when they had a pig roast and the odor permeated the neighborhood.

But that was the only time they were legally noticed.

Usually they did home contracting. Driving around they would scout out homes that needed a new driveway, siding or roof.

They would stop and ring the doorbell and point out that they did paving and roofing. Of course their price would be so low that anyone in their right mind would jump at the chance. Until they finished, that is.

It was not unusual for them to start and not finish a job. Once they got paid, they were gone.

And their work was not the best either.

There was one gypsy girl who was of marriage age. She wore a flowing multi-colored dress and had long wavy dark hair. She had a hard look to her but if you looked into her face she was really very pretty.

Sasha was walking on Broadway in Bayonne when she saw a handsome young man standing on the corner. She was mesmerized by his good looks. His tight-fitting police uniform and high cheekbones made him look like a male model.

He turned and saw her standing only a few feet from him. He smiled and said hello to her. Unlike her sisters she was not hesitant to make friends with the locals.

She was forced to go to school in New Jersey as her family had lived too long in one town, and she got to know the non-gypsy kids and became friends with them. Of course this was against both her parent's wishes and the other kids' parents also. But she actually grew to like some of them and didn't see them as future marks as her parents did.

Sasha was actually very likable, friendly, and outgoing and got along with everyone. Now she was eighteen and the young police officer caught the young girl's attention.

They started to talk and she found out he was single and only twenty-five. He had just joined the police force and this was his first year on it.

The two young people stood there talking, smiling, and even had a small laugh or two together.

Maybe they could talk again tomorrow, she thought to herself. He was very cute and she was in love for the first time.

Even though he was not a gypsy, maybe things would work out, she dreamed that night in bed. She never felt this way before.

The next morning Sasha woke up and could not wait to go to that corner and meet him again. Her heart was throbbing with excitement and anticipation.

When she awoke her mother greeted her and told her that she would be moving down south. They had arranged a marriage for her with another clan and it would bring the two families together much better prospects in the future.

It is suggested that after each story you *wait* a moment or so and think about the people you just read about before going on. Thank you.

25 - Daria

Daria had a very pretty face and you could even say she was cute. But the rest of her body was large and round. This caused her problems in her youth.

Not able to run and play with the other kids, she would internalize her feelings and start to eat. This just compounded the problem for her.

She never had a boyfriend or even a date.

Her personality was great as she was very outgoing and friendly. A kind person, she always volunteered for projects to help either people or animals.

High school was not a problem, but when she graduated she didn't know what she wanted to do. She ended up going to three community colleges until she decided that she would go to the Fashion Institute of Technology in Manhattan and study fashion design.

So Daria moved to the city and rented a room in an apartment with four other girls. Each girl had a section of the fridge for their stuff and a lock for their bedroom door.

In her room she had a weaving machine she had purchased so she could make her own sweaters and scarves. This was a large machine and other than a bed and plastic bins for her clothes, you couldn't fit anything else in it. But Daria was happy.

One night she went with some friends from school to a nightclub where only women hung out. It was there she discovered she was attracted to women.

Her feelings were that it's only skin and it doesn't matter if they are male or female. So she fell in with that crowd and had a ball.

She met this one girl from the Bronx who was a singer and they started to date. Her name was Alicia and she was half Daria's size. She was very petite and quiet when other people were present. You might even say she was shy and retiring.

How she became a singer in a rock band was beyond anyone's belief but that was what she wanted to do with her life.

The two girls decided to move in together and they rented a small apartment on the northern tip of Manhattan, almost in the Bronx.

Things were going well until they realized one worked days and the other nights. They never saw each other or if they did, one of them was tired. The relationship started to unravel not because they didn't care for each other, but they just drifted apart due to their schedules.

So Daria moved out and rented a small room again in an apartment with other girls as she had done before.

She tried to lose weight and even went to a gym and started to lose a few pounds. The weight loss started to show. Her face had slimmed down and she now had a waist. Daria also noticed that when she walked down the streets boys were starting to notice her.

It was a spring day when she was attending an interior design school and the class had a break. She walked outside to get some fresh air. Another design student, Sheila, approached her with another fellow student, Steve. He was tall, slender, and very cute.

The three started to talk and they all had a few laughs and some interesting conversations.

Finally Sheila left and it was just Daria and Steve talking about everything and about nothing.

It was at that moment that Daria switched teams.

It is suggested that after each story you _wait_ a moment or so and think about the people you just read about before going on. Thank you.

26 – Drug Bust

When the police arrived, they were wearing bulletproof vests and helmets.

They established a perimeter around the apartment complex with police on the roof above the fire escape and on the street by all the exits. No one was allowed on the street, either walking or driving.

They were after a known drug lord in Brooklyn and they were not going to let him escape.

A battering ram was brought up to the floor where they were setting up.

The preparations were almost done. Soon they would explode into the apartment and years of undercover work would pay off in the arrest of one of the biggest drug kingpins in the city.

It was almost four thirty and all their watches were synchronized. They were all to go on the half hour, exactly.

There was no room for error. They knew he was heavily armed and would not go down easily.

The captain held the search warrant in his hand.

Slowly time dragged on.

They heard Oprah on the television inside the apartment. Their information was that he watched Oprah every day and at the half hour commercial break he went to the bathroom to take a hit. He hasn't changed his habit for over a year.

The snitch was very reliable and had helped get other guys off the street in the past. He was always on the money.

Inside were three men and a woman. LaTisha was his woman and she went with him everywhere. The word was she also was armed, as well as the men inside.

The time had arrived.

Two hard knocks on the door and at the same time the captain yelled out, "Police, open up. We have a warrant."

They didn't wait for an answer and two officers battered the door in immediately.

They entered with their guns drawn, ready to open fire.

Two of the men were sitting and watching Oprah and they dropped to the floor and pulled out their guns.

It was mayhem with bullets going all over the place. The police had automatic rifles and they hit their mark.

As soon as it started, it was over.

There were two dead men on the floor and another in the next room. A bullet penetrated the thin sheetrock walls and hit its target by accident.

There were so many shots going off that the dead men's bullets went everywhere.

They didn't have time to aim.

But where was the girl?

She was missing. They knew she was in there because they heard her talking just before they went in.

Room by room they started to search for her. Guns at the ready, they tore every piece of furniture away from the walls and turned them over.

Dressers were pushed down, sofas flipped, nothing was left to chance.

"Knock on the walls," the captain shouted. "She has to be somewhere." They just couldn't figure out where.

Finally they found a fake wall that led to the apartment next door.

Rushing out the front door they battered the next apartment's door down.

Two pit bulls attacked when they entered and they shot them dead.

LaTisha was the brains behind the operation. No one knew it. Everyone took orders from her and her boyfriend relayed them as if he was the biggie.

LaTisha knew her time was up.

As the police entered the last bedroom where she was hiding, she stepped forward and placed her hand on her holstered pistol.

As they stood there facing one another, guns drawn, they knew the faceoff had to end.

LaTisha had to make a decision…was life worth living?

It is suggested that after each story you *wait* a moment or so and think about the people you just read about before going on. Thank you.

27 – Newlyweds

The wedding ceremony had ended and the party started in earnest.

An orthodox Jewish wedding is unlike any other. It took place in Williamsburg Brooklyn in the basement of a yeshiva (school).

The invited guests were over three hundred and that was just the men. The women were on the other side of a sliding wall. They celebrated in adjoining rooms.

In keeping with tradition, the newlywed couple was segregated in a locked room for one hour. There is a bed in there and they are supposed to consummate the marriage. Even in secular marriages there are two parts to a marriage. First is the ceremony, either religious or not, then the second part is the consummation of the union. If the second part is not done, there is no legal marriage (remember Mary and Joseph?).

When everything was finished, they moved to Monsey, New York, and he commuted to Manhattan every day to work in the diamond district.

Everything was going great for about a year until springtime. Then on Wednesdays he would be late getting home.

His wife started to worry.

Was he cheating on her? Why was he late getting home? Is he okay?

When asked he just said he was delayed. Then he would change the subject.

Concerned, she went to see a private investigator in Monsey.

"Could you follow my husband and see if he is cheating on me?" she asked.

The investigator usually did not do this kind of work. He worked on insurance cases but he felt sorry for this young girl who was so concerned about her husband. He said he would do his best and told her his rates, plus expenses. She agreed.

So the next Wednesday he went into the city and followed her husband as he left work and got on a bus that went from Manhattan directly to Monsey, New York.

He saw the man get off the bus about halfway to Monsey in front of a motel and walk into the motel office.

The next week the investigator parked his car in the motel parking lot and waited for the young husband to get off the bus and go into the motel.

He saw the husband go into a room. But no one else went in there with him.

The investigator waited.

Then he approached the door to the room and listened at the window to see if he heard something.

All he could hear was the television. There was no talking.

So he knocked on the door and when the husband in his underwear answered the door, he introduced himself and told him he was hired by his wife because she was very worried about him getting home late on Wednesdays.

He was not cheating o his wife, he explained.

But in the spring he enjoyed watching baseball as the orthodox do not watch television in their homes.

He always brought with him a ham sandwich and a beer while he watched the games. He couldn't do this at home.

He wasn't cheating on his wife, he was just taking a break that he really enjoyed but couldn't tell anyone.

"Please don't tell her what I do," he pleaded.

The next day the investigator called the young wife into his office and told her the following: "I can assure you that your husband is not cheating and he is fine. There is nothing to worry about. Being that I didn't have to do anything much there is no charge for my services."

With that the marriage was saved and life went on.

It is suggested that after each story you _wait_ a moment or so and think about the people you just read about before going on. Thank you.

28 – The Airplane

The airplane took off from Kennedy Airport without a problem.
It was to be a routine flight. At least that was what everyone expected.
Before takeoff the stewardess made the mandatory announcements. Seatbelts, buzzers for assistance and how to use the oxygen mask if it deployed.

Mary was the head stewardess and she had just become engaged. It would be her first marriage. She was thirty-nine and had plenty of romance in her life but never found the one that she would have liked to settle down with until now. Together they picked out her ring before she left on this flight. With deep anticipation they were now planning the wedding.

In the front of the coach section was the O'Brian family with their two children, Kathy, six, and Sean eight. They were going on a short vacation together for the first time since Kathy was born. Her red hair and freckled face spoke of her Irish ancestry.

They heard the hum of the engines as the plane reached altitude and it rattled around the cabin. But everyone was either reading or trying to grab a little sleep. It was going to be a while before they got to their destination so no one paid any attention to the noise.

The airplane was only ten years old and it had been well maintained. The seats were comfortable, though small, yet everyone felt relaxed.

Another ho hum flight.

The skies were clear as they flew over the Atlantic Ocean and if you looked out the window you only saw blue.

There were about one hundred and fifty people aboard the flight and everything was calm.

The pilot left the cockpit to use the restroom. The copilot locked the door behind him as he left. That was the protocol.

Then the plane started to nosedive.

Plates were thrown off the tray tables into people's faces. Sodas splashed onto their shirts while the food cart started to roll backwards towards the rear of the plane.

The oxygen masks came down and people panicked. Most couldn't grab the masks as the plane started to quickly spiral down.

Anyone who was not strapped into their seats started to levitate upwards. Almost like a gravity-free space walk. The stewardesses bounced against the ceiling. One was knocked unconscious and broke her front teeth against the cabin roof.

People started to yell, some cried, some held their loved ones tightly. Words of love and prayers flowed from many mouths.

The pilot blacked out when the plane started to go down because he hit his head on the lavatory walls. The space was very small.

In the cockpit the navigator held on and realized what was happening. He remembered that the copilot the other day had said how depressed he was. He was deeply in debt and saw no way out unless his life insurance paid his widow, so his family would be free of his debt.

There are no weapons on a plane anymore. But the navigator took a wrench that maintenance crews' routinely leave, opened his seatbelt, and leapt forward striking the copilot on the head knocking him unconscious.

He was also a pilot, but for smaller aircraft. This was just a bigger plane.

The navigator was not qualified by the FAA to fly this size jet but he had no choice. He jumped into the pilot's seat and tried to level off the plane.

The G force was immense. The water was fast approaching; his muscles were straining to gain control of the plane. There were only seconds left….

It is suggested that after each story you _wait_ a moment or so and think about the people you just read about before going on. Thank you.

29 – A Nun's Story

Her gold cross shined in the bright sunlight as it beamed through the church windows.

Kathy's family was there as were the families of the other two girls who were going to take their vows. It was their first vows, not their final ones.

They would have to wait a few years before they took those. The girls had to be sure that a nun's life in a convent was really for them.

All of them were devoted Catholics and were raised in church-going families and went to parochial schools all their lives.

This was the culmination of their goals in life. They believed in what they were doing.

The order they were joining was a teaching order and was very strict.

Iron gates and heavy steel doors were at the entry to the convent. Once they closed, they rarely opened for anyone to leave. If you left the convent, except for school or an emergency, the chance was you were not coming back to that lifestyle.

The mother Superior was very strict about that.

But the girls knew this and they were not looking back.

Dedicating yourself to God was their goal and they were about to take their first vows.

Kathy never dated before she entered the convent. She did go to college for two years, to get her two-year degree, where she got straight A's. But she had a calling and left to enter the convent.

This was not a stupid kid making a spontaneous decision.

While in high school she used to babysit for a Jewish family and on Saturday nights would walk to church with the children so she could go to services.

One day the children's mother, Laya, was walking past the church and the priest came by and said hello to each child by name. He saw them every Saturday night when Kathy would come with them and hang out afterwards for a short while with the nuns. The mother laughed and thought it was very funny that the priest knew her Jewish children's names.

Then it happened.

Kathy's aunt died and she was very close to her. This was her mother's sister and she wasn't sure if the convent would let her leave to attend the funeral. She was only in the convent for six months or so and was very upset over this.

But they did let her out for the funeral with a chaperone.

She stopped by the Jewish family's house she babysat for to say hello before she left again.

She told Laya that if they didn't let her attend the funeral she would have left the order.

At that moment, Laya knew that Kathy would not stay in the convent and she would eventually leave.

As time went on, Laya moved out of town with her family and she lost touch with Kathy's mother and the other folks on the block where she had lived.

It wasn't until twenty some-odd years had passed that Laya met someone who was from the old town she had moved from and knew Kathy.

She was told that Kathy did leave the convent, met a young man, got married, and now has six children of her own.

It is suggested that after each story you _wait_ a moment or so and think about the people you just read about before going on. Thank you.

30 – NYC Councilman

It was a sunny summer morning just before noon. A cool breeze was blowing in from the East River and gently kissing the face of whomever was outside in City Hall Park in Manhattan.

The mayor walked out of city hall and slowly went down the front stairs to get in his limo when he was called back for an emergency.

Inside Councilman Joe Hailings had just shot another councilman in city hall.

Police came running into the building with their guns drawn and went directly back to the council chambers.

There stood the gunman holding a pistol to his head.

Everyone ran out of the room as the police came dashing in. They stopped at the door and saw the body lying on the floor in a pool of blood. The gun was not pointed at them so they held their fire. They backed out waiting for a commander to show up and take charge.

Hailings was told to relax, take it easy. Stay calm. A sergeant was doing the talking until a higher office came.

Tears started to trickle down Joe's cheeks as he stood there with a gun to his head. He had loved the man he shot.

Last night, after three years together, they had an extremely severe argument and broke up. It was a lover's quarrel that needlessly went too far.

The wounds were obviously very deep and carried over to the next day at work.

Both men had been activists in New York not only for gay rights but for their neighborhood also. That was how they met.

Joe was elected to represent his district and his lover was an at-large councilman. This afforded them the opportunity to live together in the same voting district.

His lover was a great speaker and used his words as a weapon. His wit was sharp and to the point. He knew that a word could do as much damage as a knife or gun. Once spoken it cannot be put back into a sheath or holster.

That night the words were spoken with deadly accuracy and they found its mark on Joe Hailings' heart and mind.

The mental pain was terrible and he couldn't bear to even remember what was said. But his mind kept repeating those arrows to his heart and he cracked under the stress.

When he woke the next morning he was alone. His lover had left last night and went to a hotel in the city until he could send for his clothes.

Devastated on losing the love of his life, Joe knew where he could buy an illegal handgun. He took some cash he had in the apartment and bought one from someone he was told about in a gay club.

He didn't even know if it worked or how to use it. He had never handled a gun before.

A captain arrived and started to talk to him to calm down. Don't make it worse, he was told.

Joe was not thinking straight. His mind was not interpreting what his ears were hearing.

Confused.

He remembered what Boy George had once said, "There is no such thing as bad love." But this was bad love because it hurt him. "Things were going well, what happened?" he thought to himself. He just couldn't comprehend the event that brought him here, now.

He couldn't believe that after all those years together he was being left for someone else.

It didn't matter that he was gay or not. People fall in and out of love all the time.

He just couldn't handle it.

It is suggested that after each story you *wait* a moment or so and think about the people you just read about before going on. Thank you.

66

31 - Ella

She was born in the hill country of West Virginia in a small town with no traffic lights.

The place had a gray tinge to it, like shadows, and was quite dreary looking.

But there was one house on the fringe of town that was painted yellow and green with lavender trim. It stood out, and inside it was as cheerful as the exterior.

The Clancy family lived there and their only daughter Ella had inherited the cheerfulness of the family. She was a light in the darkness.

Throughout her school years she was the flame to the moths. All the kids were drawn to her by her personality and charm.

Never a great beauty, but a nice-looking girl, she always was courted and she never had to wait for a boy to ask her out.

After high school she was accepted at the University of Virginia on a scholarship. She had decided that the world was not a very peaceful place so she studied political science. The state department was her goal.

A career in the diplomatic service could possibly give her the opportunity to make a meaningful contribution to peace.

She interned in Washington, D.C., as a senior and after graduation was offered a full-time, temporary position with the state department. Ella had a mentor whom she worked under who saw to it she was appointed to a job under his supervision.

As her mentor moved up through the years she followed and was finally hired as a full-time civil servant in the department. Her first posting was as an assistant to the ambassador in Mumbai, India.

She was there for two years and traveled all around India during her time off.

The mass of poor people in India seemed to attract her to them. It reminded her of the townsfolk back in West Virginia.

She worked in her spare time in an orphanage trying to set up a liaison with an American adoption agency. Her hope was that maybe if even one child was given the American opportunity to succeed, she would have done a good deed.

Ella was getting more involved in her charity work and making good contacts, both for her adoption agency goal and also for her career.

The ambassador was very fond of her as she was always cheerful and outgoing. This was a stark contrast to the reserved Indian diplomatic way as it was a leftover from the British way of doing things.

There was a small dinner in the Crystal Room at one of the best hotels in Mumbai. The ambassador had a previous engagement and asked Ella if she could please represent him there.

The room was amazing. It had crystal chandeliers, hand-carved baroque woodwork, and unbelievable silk-lined walls. Elegant was an understatement.

Only the music was subdued.

Ella mingled and was always engaged in a conversation. She was the ambassador's representative at the dinner and everyone wanted to speak with her.

Things were going well. She had made a contact for her orphanage and also met a high-ranking Indian diplomat who hit it off with her.

They had decided to meet the following week to talk about things in general.

Just then there was gunfire and explosions just outside the door to the Crystal Room.

People ran for an exit but when they opened the door they were shot.

It was November 2008 and terrorists had stormed the hotel on a suicide mission.

Ella was trapped in the Taj Mahal Palace and Tower hotel….

It is suggested that after each story you *wait* a moment or so and think about the people you just read about before going on. Thank you.

32 - Juan

I had worked in a large metropolitan hospital as an art therapist in the pediatric wing for a many years.

My main function was to help these children deal with their pain using art as a vehicle. Here are a few cases that I was working on.

I remember Juanita when she came into my wing. She was eight years old and had been in and out of the hospital for years battling cancer. Juanita was on her last protocol and it was not working.

Her mother could not deal with the situation and abandoned the family two years ago.

All Juanita had left was her devoted father, Juan, who came every day before and after work to see his beloved daughter.

If there was a procedure that was to be done on her, Juan would take off from work to be with her. This caused him to lose his job. Then he was evicted from his apartment for non-payment of rent.

When the doctors felt that there was very little time left for her, Juan stayed with her twenty-four hours a day. Juan was now homeless and the nurses let him sleep on a cot in the room with her until she died.

The staff started a collection in the hospital to pay for her funeral.

Juan was heartbroken, homeless, and had nowhere to go.

The social worker at the hospital arranged for him to be employed by, and drive a van for, the hospital. She also arranged for a one-room apartment for him to stay, and had furniture donated by a local business.

The father saw me in the hall and stopped to thank me for the art project I did with his daughter. She was suffering from sickle cell anemia and would be in great pain. He said I had really helped her and he appreciated what I did.

I had her draw a picture of a tree where she imagined she could go and be free of pain. Then I had her draw a door. I cut out the door on three sides so she could open it and look at the tree if she was in pain. This caused her relief when the pain would start.

The head nurse in the PIC unit (pediatric intensive care) asked me one day to teach her how I did the hand and foot prints.

I mixed special clay and when an infant would die of SIDS they would call me down to the unit. I then pressed their tiny hands and feet into the clay and write the infant's name on it. When it dried I would present it to the parents as a keepsake of their baby.

The parents had to request this. But it had to be done quickly before the body stiffened, otherwise I could break a bone (I never did).

One evening at dinner I was telling my parents about my day and my father, after drying his tears, asked me not to discuss the day's events until after we ate.

The story that upset him so much was about Angela.

She was five years old and was dying of cancer.

That day her mother was with her and I was in the room also. She looked up at her mother and asked her how long it takes, once she goes to heaven, until she gets her wings.

That was the final straw for my father.

And I didn't even tell him about my part-time position at night doing pediatric grief counseling!

It is suggested that after each story you *wait* a moment or so and think about the people you just read about before going on. Thank you.

33 - Andrea

She woke up one day and decided she had to turn her life around.

Being in the county jail awaiting trial was not where she had intended to end up when she left home at seventeen.

Her parents believed in tough love and refused to bail her out. She would call collect every day and beg her parents to bail her out.

In jail she would drew pictures of the other inmate's children for the women and they said they would have it tattooed once they got out of jail.

Andrea ran away from home with her drug addict boyfriend, Daren. They had stolen her mother's car and took off on a burglary spree to feed both of their heroin habits.

They drove around New Jersey, and even ventured into Pennsylvania, breaking into homes to steal gold jewelry to sell.

Daren would kick in the either the back door, or the front if no one was around, and run upstairs and ransack the master bedroom.

Once he even stole a gun from a home but Andrea yelled at him and he threw it away in some woods that they drove past.

Sleeping in the car, eating a diet of fast food, and shooting up was their lifestyle.

Finally they were caught on a traffic violation, stopped, and arrested.

Daren already had a police record and would be convicted and sentenced to five years in prison.

Andrea's parents had hired a lawyer to defend her. They were both teachers and hired a public defender from a neighboring town that was recommended to them. He knew how to talk to the courts.

That was a good thing as they were wanted in five jurisdictions. In New Jersey being convicted of three felonies could mean a life sentence. But the public defender spoke to each judge, in each trial, and was able to get all arrests merged into one.

Her parents had to pay to get her into a long-term rehab center where she stayed for almost one year. This was in lieu of prison as the judges all agreed to this.

When she got out of the rehab she got a job working at night till midnight at a hotel as the switchboard operator. She was able to save over three thousand dollars working at seven dollars an hour.

She then went to school to be a beautician and got her license to cut hair.

There was no way she would be going back to jail. She spent over ninety days in the county lockup and that put the fear of the Lord in her. Andrea was only a little over five feet five and one hundred pounds (due to her heroin addiction). Petite and tiny was not a good thing to be in jail and she didn't want to go back. She was exposed to tuberculosis in there and became a carrier. When she got out she was treated for it at a clinic.

Once she got her cosmetology license, she got a job in a beauty salon in a nearby town.

Then one day a tall, good-looking fellow came in with his son to have their hair cut. The son talked to her and eventually asked her out.

Andrea started to date this young man and they went out for a few months.

He told his mother after the first date he felt he was going to marry Andrea.

It took almost a year but they did get married.

Within the first year they had a baby and moved into their own apartment.

She had turned her life around.

It is suggested that after each story you _wait_ a moment or so and think about the people you just read about before going on. Thank you.

34 - Alone

The helicopter landed in the middle of a field. The gunner was looking for any activity in the tree line about fifty feet away.

It was a tight landing but that's where they wanted them to go. They were to move through the jungle to relieve a unit that was holding a small hillside.

Late May in Vietnam was not a picnic. The temperature was about ninety-five and very humid. But here, they were with their backpacks and supplies about to track through South Vietnam jungle.

The threat of an ambush was on everyone's mind. The Cong knew they were coming. They wouldn't stop attacking the base camp and knew that reinforcements would be showing up eventually.

The sergeant was in another base camp previously and he said it was the scariest thing when they attacked.

He told them that you can hear them screaming. Then the gunfire started and out of the jungle comes hundreds of naked Viet Cong wearing just ammo belts and high on drugs. The sweat gleamed in the sun and just dripped off their bodies. This made them very hard to fight in close quarters as there was nothing to grab on them. The sweat was like grease and made them very slippery.

Yelling and shooting, they just kept coming. They were so high that even if you shot them they just continued coming at you. They felt no pain. You had to shoot them in the heart or head or they just continued running at you.

The sergeant told them he could swear he killed one but he just got closer and closer and jumped on him and tried to kill him with a knife. Finally the sergeant said he just kept shooting him with his pistol at point blank range until he slacked off of him.

As they entered by the tree line the sergeant called for one of the new men in the unit to take the point. They had discovered a small trail and would follow it.

The soldier walked up to the head of the line and started to walk on the path. The others stayed back about twenty feet as he started to go forward.

He knew it was dangerous.

At that time he felt very alone, almost naked.

Landmines were probably planted on the path. Thin trip wires attached to explosives couldn't be seen in the heavy underbrush.

This was just like Russian roulette, but playing for keeps.

He was drafted into the army from high school and really didn't want to be here. But he didn't want to run away from his responsibilities as he saw them.

Yet here he was. The sweat was starting to run down his face. His stomach was in a knot from nerves. All he could do was walk forward and look down.

He couldn't think of anything else except to focus on the ground. His life was dependent on his luck and eyesight. But there really was no way a person could see the planted mines. They were covered really well.

The hospital in Saigon could attest to that fact.

Every few feet he would stop and listen. He hoped that he would hear something that would warn him. He would rather be in a fire fight because he felt at least then he had a chance. But being the point in a jungle war was not the way to have a long life.

But he was a United States soldier and he was not going to let down his buddies.

So he took the next step....

It is suggested that after each story you _wait_ a moment or so and think about the people you just read about before going on. Thank you.

35 - Shanice

She walked with confidence, holding her head high and straight. Her eyes did not wander from side to side as she crossed the street on Broadway. The light was green for her and she led the crowd onto the black asphalt.

Shanice was not a natural beauty in the world of fashion, but she knew how to put herself together and was striking to look at.

She was tall and thin and the colors of her clothes just complemented her color perfectly.

At twenty-eight she was an executive at a high-powered public relations firm in Manhattan. Her clientele were the high profile people of New York and Washington.

She had worked her way up to this position with her ability to meet and know the right people, and what to say both to them and for them.

It wasn't unusual to see her on the arm of a famous celebrity having lunch at 21. That was part of her job. And she made sure the right people were there to see both her and her client.

Often her clients would be quoted in the newspaper the next day after having met with her.

Her black hair was straightened and cut in layers and just seemed to flow as her head turned.

The makeup she used was custom colored for her skin tone, by appointment, at a very exclusive studio on Madison Avenue.

When you looked at her you saw success.

Shanice took nothing for granted and knew where she came from.

Her father was a bus driver in Manhattan until he retired and her mother used to clean homes for white people while she was growing up. She had two older brothers who had left home years ago. One was in the army and the other moved to the west coast to try and get into the movie business.

Shanice had almost everything she had wanted to attain in life. But she was still missing one thing.

As an educated black girl she succeeded in a white world. There were few black men around she knew that were her equal. Most of them had already either married, were dating, gay, or otherwise taken. And most of the taken were with white girls. She didn't date white.

Her firm had just taken on a hospital in Manhattan that was about to expand. They needed some professional PR to help them with the politicians and to help get state and city funding. She knew everyone and was assigned to the client.

When she went to the hospital she was given an escorted tour of the current facilities. They wanted her to know what they wanted to do and why.

When she went into the research department she was introduced to a very handsome, young, black doctor that was working there.

For the first time in a long time she didn't know exactly what to say. His blue eyes contrasted against his dark skin and she thought he was beautiful.

At first she didn't recognize his accent. He was foreign born but he spoke perfect English and seemed to be very outgoing and friendly to her.

Could this be the one, she thought?

She asked him if he would like to have dinner with her that evening. He said he would like to very much.

At dinner she found out he was an Ethiopian Jew from Israel and was here on a work visa.

He was everything she had wanted in a man.

Her mind raced. This might be the one.

They need PR people in Israel too!

It is suggested that after each story you _wait_ a moment or so and think about the people you just read about before going on. Thank you.

36 – K.A.C. Crib

He went to a local college in the South. It was not a noteworthy school but served a purpose in the rural area where it was located.

Derik was a local boy who got a job at the largest company in his small town, The K.A.C. Crib Company, after graduation

He married a local girl, had children, and bowled in the company bowling league with the other employees. He was just one of the guys.

The company was growing and had a national reputation due to its quality and marketing. It believed in advertising and had ads in all the national family magazines.

He was working his way up the ladder in management. The headquarters was located about an hour away from any major city. They were limited to hiring local people due to its location in the middle of nowhere.

As the years went along, Derik's eye for the ladies eventually earned him a divorce and he was now free to date openly. As if that ever stopped him.

Then the company hired a new sales manager, Tad Cramden, who came from a much larger crib company. He had built up a network of baby stores for that company and was hired to help K.A.C. Crib grow also.

The first thing he did was promote Derik to be the assistant sales manager.

When Tad wanted something done, he instructed Derik on how to do it and Derik saw that it got done. Derik became the hatchet man in the company.

Tad hired an advertising manager for K.A.C. and changed the look of the ads.

A rivalry developed between the new ad man and Derik.

A national advertising agency was hired from Atlanta to do its promotions and the vice president of the agency would often meet at K.A.C. offices with the advertising manager and then she would drive back to Atlanta.

The rollout of the new franchised K.A.C. Baby Galleries was a hit when they were introduced. They even licensed a line of baby clothes to sell in their stores and other proprietary goods also.

Eventually they bought a few clothing companies to bring under their advertising umbrella.

But then the problems started.

The stores they allowed to open had to be in triple A locations with very high rents. Stores started to fail.

There wasn't enough volume to cover the high rents and fixed costs.

The advertising manager left for an electronics manufacturer.

Derik eventually became national sales manager.

Derik was seen having lunch with the VP of the advertising agency even though he was now married and had nothing to do with the companies ads.

The ads got stale but there was now a relationship with the agency and they didn't seek a new one.

By now they were on listed on the American Stock Exchange and were thinking of moving up to the big board.

But sales started to fall. Stores closed. Profits tanked.

In a desperate effort the company started to take over the failed stores. They knew nothing about running a retail operation.

Their cribs were now overpriced and the company was trading on their name as a quality crib manufacturer. But it was not enough.

Target, Babies R Us, and others carried baby items and cribs now.

In a desperate move K.A.C. moved their manufacturing to China to cut costs.

But they were late to the game and couldn't find an available quality manufacturer.

Their quality suffered and they were not leaders anymore, but followers.

Two years later the name was sold and they were closed.

It is suggested that after each story you *wait* a moment or so and think about the people you just read about before going on. Thank you.

37 - Dad

I received the phone call about noontime. I didn't expect to hear my wife tell me Dad is very ill and was taken to the hospital this morning.

She thought I should leave work now and go see him. There was a nervous type of sadness in her voice. I sensed that something was really wrong and left immediately.

Driving over the Verrazano Bridge I remember thinking how bright the sun was shining. It was a beautiful October day and I was not used to driving at midday, only in the early morning and late rush hours.

How could he be in the hospital on such a nice day?

When I arrived I was directed to the Cardiac Intensive Care Unit.

My wife and mother were with him. He was just lying there covered with blankets, so many blankets. They were trying to warm him, to warm his feet.

He had an aneurysm by the heart and it was critical.

I tried to kid around with him as he was awake and responsive. It was small talk but he answered me. His great sense of humor was still active and alive. He was kidding with me even now as he lay in the ICC unit.

I went back in to see him before they wheeled him into the operating room.

At the time I was forty years old and had a great relationship with my father.

A day didn't go by that I didn't call him to talk to him, seek his advice, or even argue with him. He always forgave me, too.

If I got mad and hung up on him he would call me back and say he accepts my apology. How could you argue with a man who forgives you before you say you're sorry! In all those forty years we had a great understanding of each other.

He was honest and aboveboard in all his dealings in life. He saw humor that eluded others and he saw the same humor that they saw also was known for his huge belly laugh.

Now, in the small cubicle that they placed him in, with the pale green hospital walls and curtains surrounding him, I alone was the last one with him. The nurses came to put him on the gurney and then they parted the curtains I thought, "This might be the final goodbye."

I kissed my father on the cheek as I often did. He kissed his father all the time and I kissed my father all the time. I now kiss my two sons also.

There is nothing unmasculine in showing true affection.

Yet, something bothered me. In forty years, with all the affection and love he gave to me and that I gave to him, I felt I had to do one last thing for him.

The cart was moving now, slowly. I walked beside him.

I bent over for one last kiss on the cheek and told him something I had never said to him in all my life. "I love you," I whispered in his ear after the kiss. "I know you do," he said, and smiled to me as they wheeled him away to the operating room.

When I told my children that Grandpa had died that night my youngest daughter, who was seven years old asked, "Did he die from laughing too much?"

What a warm way to be remembered.

It is suggested that after each story you *wait* a moment or so and think about the people you just read about before going on. Thank you.

38 - Aliens

Somewhere in the Midwest the government has radio wave telescopes beaming signals into space looking for alien life.

This has been going on for decades with no luck in finding any. Then one day they received a signal back. They can't believe their eyes. They looked at the electroscopes and saw radio signals coming in.

A life-form is sending out radio signals to earth!

The supervisor called Washington and informed them of the signals.

They decide to try to decode what was beaming in.

Finally the Hubble telescope picked up visual signals.

The astronomers' figured it would take a few months before it arrived.

The electricity that was running through the halls of Washington could be felt.

What do they want? Where are they coming from? Where will they land? Are they peaceful?

Nobody knows the answers.

The president had meetings all day long with his national security advisors and with the heads of NASA.

Governments from all over the world are curious and are trying to find out more information from the United States.

Either people are panicking from fear of the unknown or are excited waiting to see what is coming.

Sidewalk preachers are forecasting the end of the world. The human race could be food for the aliens, some are saying. Just as we eat cattle, they will eat us.

Rumors flowed from people who knew nothing.

Finally the President of the United States went on television and spoke to the world.

He told everyone that we were able to decipher some of the signals from the object hurtling towards Earth.

The scientists were able to make out an object and that signals were being sent to us.

It appeared to be a white dove holding a branch.

The president said that the scientists he consulted with feel that the space craft is not hostile.

He also spoke with Russian, French, and British scientists and they all felt the same way.

As he spoke more signals were coming in and they were learning how to decipher them.

It was not an easy thing to do.

The signals were being sent in code. Dots and dashes very similar to Morse code but yet different.

The main frame computers at the Pentagon were trying to understand them. They were working twenty-four hours a day on this project. The scientists had to make sure there was a peaceful intent.

This was going to be a first meeting with an alien life-form. There was no knowledge of how they looked or exactly what they wanted.

Finally they made a breakthrough and were able to understand everything that was being sent to Earth. They were writing in a variable of an extremely ancient language.

It seems they were here before. Many times, and many eons ago, and had left some signs behind them. But they were not found.

They said that they had even left some of their species on earth to populate and colonize the planet for future settlement.

But no one knew what they looked like.

Finally they landed in a desert area of New Mexico.

The military were there waiting as well as scientists.

Their craft had a small door that opened and a few of the space creatures walked out.

They appeared to have a humanoid form.

Dressed in reflective black clothes they also had short hair but wore long beards.

The Vice President of the United States approached to welcome them to Earth.

He extended his hand in a peaceful motion.

The alien looked him in the eye.

They stood only a few feet apart, motionless, for a moment.

Finally the space visitor opened his mouth and said… "Shalom."

It is suggested that after each story you _wait_ a moment or so and think about the people you just read about before going on. Thank you.

39 – Las Vegas

The young couple, Alex and Jill, was on their honeymoon in Las Vegas and went to see a show at the Riviera Hotel.

The headliner was Sammy Davis Junior and it was the late show. When they walked into the main room the maître d' took them to a booth in the rear. The Alex asked if there was a better seat available and slipped a ten dollar bill into the hand of the maître d'.

He took them to a table next to the stage.

The music started and an opening act came out.

It was a dance group and the girls were spectacular. They bounced around the stage with their hair done up and smiles as wide as the Grand Canyon.

When they were finished there was a short break and the announcer introduced the main act.

Sammy came out and started to sing. He was great. Dancing, singing, and talking to the audience like they were long lost friends.

Some of the dancers came out to see the show after they had changed. Their wigs were off and they just sat quietly, smoked, had a drink, and watched the show.

Afterwards they went to the Diplomat Hotel for a bite to eat. They had a cafeteria where you put money in a slot, opened the door, and took your food out.

It was self-serve, the tables had Formica tops, and the chairs were just plain dining chairs on a tiled floor.

The main dishes were handed to you from behind glass by servers standing behind a glass divider. You then took the dish of food and placed it on your tray.

As they sat down to eat they saw a bridal party of five sitting and eating at another table. This was their wedding dinner.

The bride was still in her gown, the groom in his tuxedo, and the others in suits and a dress.

When they were finished eating they went into the casino to gamble a little.

Alex and Jill didn't have a lot of money to be spent in the casino so they went to the slot machines and started to insert their quarters.

Alex went through his five dollars and had nothing to show for it.

Jill was winning. Her machine went off lots of times. The bells sounded, coins dropped into the tray hitting the metal and making the dinging sound of quarters falling en- mass.

She had won twenty-five dollars and they decided to go back to their motel and save the money.

On her way out of the casino there was a platform with a new Ford Mustang on it. There were slot machines all around the stage and if you hit the jackpot you won the car.

Alex wanted to try to win the car. He put in four quarters and pulled the lever.

Quickly the four wheels spun with the symbols whizzing past the glass window of the machine.

When the wheels stopped he had lost.

Jill wanted to try her luck. She had just won the money anyway and maybe this was her lucky night.

She sat down next to a large obese woman who was sweating a lot and smelled. This woman was not the least bit appealing but that was the only open seat available.

Jill put her money in and pulled the handle.

When it stopped she had won five dollars. She collected the quarters, got up, and left.

The large woman leaned over, put in four quarters, and pulled the handle on Jill's machine.

Bells went off....

It is suggested that after each story you *wait* a moment or so and think about the people you just read about before going on. Thank you.

40 – New ....

This state used to be a great place to live.

It boarded another state that had a major city where there were businesses, jobs, and entertainment to be had within an easy drive.

In this state there was a mayor of a large township who was trying to move up the political ladder.

Ramona McNeal was the first female mayor of a major town in that state. Plus she was of Latin and Irish heritage. A winning combination if there ever was one in contemporary politics.

A major franchise wanted to open in the city but had to go for a site plan variance.

They hired a local engineer who had worked as the city engineer for ten years and knew who to go to for answers.

He also knew what lawyer to use. The one he recommended was married to the secretary of the planning board.

Both had fees that were just slightly higher than usual, for obvious reasons.

But they got things through that otherwise might not.

So the building was being built and then the building inspectors came in.

They found the most obscure violations. It became apparent that they wanted to be paid off.

But this was a franchise for a New York Stock Exchange company and they would not play the game that way.

So the electrical inspector said he wanted the wiring that was already done brought up to next year's code. Even though the plans had been approved before construction started. It cost eleven thousand dollars to make the "corrections."

This is what Ramona had going for her in the township. She drove a very expensive car and was dating the inspector.

She decided to run for the U.S. Senate one year and almost made it. She had the backing of the reform contingent in her party and she said all the right things that the people wanted to hear.

But she lost in the primary by a hair's width but got tremendous name recognition.

After two more years she ran for governor of her state.

She said she would lower property taxes, fix the highways, lower the income tax, and eliminate the sales tax.

When she won the election she raised the income tax, raised the cigarette tax, was involved in "kick-back" scandals, and made appointments to important state posts based on personal favors, pay to play schemes, and other political paybacks.

Once elected all the reform promises she made were totally forgotten.

The thing that forced her to resign was when she had tried to make her lover, Marie Ocho, deputy finance supervisor to the governor at a salary of $125,000 per year. Considering she was not even a high school graduate, that hit the news like a lightning bolt. And she was a Dominican citizen too!

Marie was a striking woman with jet black hair and wore tight clothes to show off her figure. Her picture was all over the Internet and national news.

Finally Ramona decided that she could no longer govern as everyone was up in arms about her failings.

She met with the senate president and they worked out a plan for her to resign from the governorship.

They set up an arrangement where she would resign and the senate president, who would then be governor, would appoint her to as a judicial executive in the court system. There she could collect a salary and not be in the crosshairs of the media.

Ramona quietly faded into obscurity in a courthouse, and did nothing else.

Ousted politicians don't die, they get appointed.

It is suggested that after each story you *wait* a moment or so and think about the people you just read about before going on. Thank you.

41 - Suzanne

Suzanne was extremely charming and outgoing. She got along well with everyone she met. Some people could even say she was a natural politician in that she made friends so easily.

Growing up in rural Sussex County New Jersey, she was the high school cheerleader and student body president.

Her grades were above average though not superior and her perky attitude helped her along.

After graduation she decided to join the Army instead of going to college.

So now she was in boot camp and all the harassment that goes into making a soldier from a civilian.

There was one fellow female soldier who started to tease her and make fun of her outgoing personality.

One week they were on a three-day hike in the woods. Suzanne and this other girl were to separate from the rest and look for a campsite.

As they were climbing over a fallen tree that overlooked a cliff, Suzanne "tripped" into the other girl and sent her flying down a thirty-foot embankment.

She broke two legs and an arm and was sent to the base hospital for over two months.

Suzanne felt no remorse. In her mind she deserved it.

When Suzanne was finally stationed at a base in Texas she met a young soldier and married him.

They really didn't know each other that well but Suzanne wanted to move out of the barracks. This way she qualified for a base apartment. Love never entered the equation.

One day her husband went to the base hospital as he was feeling ill. They ran tests on him and they were negative.

A month later he was dead. The autopsy found nothing.

Suzanne collected widow's benefits and after her enlistment was over she moved to New York City.

She got a job as a personal assistant to an older wealthy woman who was also a realtor. She was to live in the maid's room of this woman's apartment.

Wanting to ensure that she would not be fired or thrown out she began a friendship with her son. Eventually it got to the point where they decided they should marry. No one knew of her first marriage.

They moved to Westchester and bought a huge mansion. The Mercedes followed as well as the unlimited credit cards.

After a few years she suspected her husband was having an affair. When confronted he admitted it and wanted a divorce.

She asked him if he had told anyone else about his wanting a divorce, and he said not yet.

She made dinner for them both and they went to their separate bedrooms.

He never woke up the next morning.

Suzanne inherited everything he had. She was now very wealthy.

She decided that New York was too cold in winter and wanted to move to Florida where the weather was warmer, the men were retired and rich, and she could start over.

Coral Gables has some beautiful homes on the water and that's where she moved.

Suzanne joined an exclusive country club to meet eligible rich men.

At a casual get-together one day she met a man who was very tall and handsome. It was rumored he had inherited his money from his father who had a banana plantation in Costa Rica.

He was educated in the states and spoke English with a very minor accent.

They started to date and eventually married.

She was hoping for another rich score, but he was not that wealthy.

In fact he wasn't wealthy at all.

One night after dinner they went to bed. Suzanne was not feeling well....

It is suggested that after each story you *wait* a moment or so and think about the people you just read about before going on. Thank you.

42 – The Bridge

The George Washington Bridge is one of the busiest bridges in the world. It has over one hundred million vehicles a year's traverse over it, nonstop.
 But today one car did stop. It stopped about midway and the driver got out.
 He walked over to the railing and put one leg over it. He stopped and looked down.
 Depression took over his thoughts as he froze sitting atop the bridge. He had no desire to live.
 It started about a year before when he and his partner were called to a disturbance at a local bar.
 They were not the only police car to arrive at the scene before the shooting started.
 The patrons were streaming out yelling that there were two men in there with guns.
 The police stopped traffic and then two of them ran into the building while the people were running out.
 Once inside they saw a man standing in the shadows, leaning against the wall, with his hand holding something dark. The lighting was low and it was hard to see. Upon warning the man they were police he picked his hand up and shakily pointed it towards them.
 They shot him in the chest and he died on the spot.
 He was holding a darkened liquor glass and not a gun. He was unarmed.

 After the inquiry both officers were found not liable for their actions.
 But one of them took it to heart.
 He was an African American officer and the young man he shot was also, and only twenty-one.
 The office was devastated. He had killed a young man the same age as his kid brother.
 That boy could have been his brother had he been there.
 It's tough to have a conscience, to have empathy for someone else when you are a police officer, and are sworn to uphold the law. Sometimes

you have to do things you don't like but are placed in a position that there is no choice.

He understood that. But it bothered him. It ate at him every night when he went to bed.

The police department sent him for counseling but it did not help. The depression just kept getting worse.

He started to lose weight, call out sick, and eventually was given time off with pay. They understood the trauma he had and were willing to help him.

But it was not enough.

Here he was, looking down from the bridge, with nothing but despair in his heart.

Cars stopped behind his. Others swerved around and kept going.

A Chevy with some young men in it, with rolled up sleeves and cigarettes dangling from their mouth, slowed down and yelled for him to jump.

It seemed like an eternity but eventually the police came on the scene and one officer started to talk to him.

But the words just went into the air and didn't penetrate his mind.

There was nothing anyone could do to save him from himself.

For just one more time, before he would place his other leg over the railing, he looked up into the sky.

The blue was beautiful with just a few high clouds floating above. It was a gorgeous day and he glanced into the sky for a last look.

He had decided that life was too painful.

In one cloud he saw something.

It looked like the holy mother, Mary holding the baby Jesus, and she was looking straight at him.

He took this as a heavenly sign to him.

Carefully he got back down onto the pavement, sat down, and openly wept.

It is suggested that after each story you *wait* a moment or so and think about the people you just read about before going on. Thank you.

43 - Izzy

It was seven in the evening and bedtime for Izzy. She was in her pj's and ready for sleep. Her mother tucked her in, turned off the lights, and kissed her goodnight before leaving the room.

Izzy was only five and she was very bright and outgoing.

There are unexplained things in life that adults can't explain. And tonight one of those things happened to bounce into Izzy's bedroom.

It was a small thump. Not loud enough to wake her parents down the hallway. But it did wake Izzy up.

She sat up and in the glow of her night light she saw Herman. He was a big rolly polly blue kangaroo with a huge smile on his face.

"Hey Izzy," he said. "Let's go out and see what's doing."

So she got out of bed, climbed into his belly pouch, and with one BIG bounce they were out of the house.

"I'm hungry," said Herman. Izzy agreed so he took one more big bounce and they landed on the boardwalk in Wildwood, New Jersey.

Amazingly no one noticed them. Herman had that strange effect on people.

He went over to a candy stand and asked if they could have some cotton candy. Izzy took the pink and Herman the blue. It blended with his fur.

"Mmmm," they both said as they ate it.

Izzy pointed to the Ferris wheel and they both decided it would be fun to go on the ride.

So with one BIG bounce they ended up in an empty car at the top of the ride. Izzy was thrilled. The view was great. She could see the ocean and almost the whole boardwalk all lit up at night.

After the ride they decided to walk a little on the boards.

There were thousands of people out that night. It was summer and a soft breeze was blowing in from the ocean cooling things off.

While they were walking they saw a little boy in a wheelchair. His legs were in braces and his parents were pushing him as they were trying to maneuver the chair through the crowds.

Izzy said to Herman, "Wouldn't it be great if that boy could walk? He could get around easier."

So Herman went over to the family. They were resting near the railing overlooking the beach.

Only the little boy could see Herman. He just looked up at him and stared. He didn't know what to say, or do.

Herman bent down and told the boy to say a small prayer for whatever he would like. Herman heard the boy's short prayer.

He took the boy's words of prayer in his blue hands and blew them to the heavens above.

Then he and Izzy stood back and watched.

The boy asked his parents if he could try to stand up. He was able to. Then he started to walk. And then he started to walk even better. He took off his braces and he was fine.

Herman was so happy for him.

But it was getting late and Izzy had to get back home.

So with one BIG bounce they landed back on her front lawn.

Unfortunately the sprinklers were on and they both got very wet.

It was getting late now. So with another bounce they were both back in her bedroom.

Izzy changed her clothes, climbed into her bed, and sat up and waved goodbye to Herman.

He tiptoed over to her and gently kissed her on the cheek and wished her pleasant dreams.

Then with a BIG bounce he was gone.

Until next time….

It is suggested that after each story you *wait* a moment or so and think about the people you just read about before going on. Thank you.

44 – Rabbi Darke

Religion is supposed to be a way to lead an ethical and moral life. It really doesn't matter which religion it is.

Rabbi Darke was hired to lead a very large congregation in a suburb of Chicago. He was a very educated person and a good speaker.

He was a rabbi in Atlanta for a few years. His congregation was a medium size and they had opened their homes and hearts to him. He had a wife and three children who just loved it there.

Everything was going great until Hurricane Katrina hit New Orleans.

People were fleeing from the flooded city and going literally escaping to any city that would take them in and aid them.

Chicago did its part and so did Rabbi Darke.

He arranged for two Jewish families to relocate to his community and he helped them settle in.

Through the use of his discretionary funds account that the synagogue had set up for such things, he was able to get them housing, clothes, and food.

Most synagogues have a discretionary account that the rabbi can use for needs that are not budgeted for. Such as paying a mortgage for a destitute family, a school trip for the Hebrew school, and other sundries and sometimes important needs without asking anyone. Just to be able to help when there is a need.

One of the families was a single woman with two children. He befriended her and helped them as much as he could.

Then when his contract was almost up, he and his wife decided to move to Atlanta to a slightly larger synagogue.

He was a jovial person and his wife was very much the outgoing rabbi's wife. She got involved in sisterhood activities and even taught in the adult education classed there. They settled in and really enjoyed living in Atlanta.

The first year went okay.

Then things started to happen.

A torah was missing. They are usually not counted as there are only a few in each synagogue, maybe two to four. Ten are a lot. They are usually valued at up to fifty thousand dollars each and are kept under lock and key.

The board of trustees hushed it up and put a claim in with the insurance company. Nobody knew where it went.

Then the year-end accounting was done. No one knew exactly to whom or for what the money was spent on in the discretionary account. Just the opening and closing balance was accounted for.

At the year end, there was always money in the account. The expenditures were always balanced with donations to the fund so there was always some money in it. This year it was empty.

Upon investigation it seems that the rabbi had paid to move the single woman and her kids to Atlanta to be near him. He was having an affair and that was why they had moved from Chicago. His wife wanted to get away from her.

With the fund's money he sent his kids and the woman's kids to summer camp, paid for private schools, and even an expensive engagement ring for the woman.

Upon this discovery he was discharged and got a job selling used cars.

The woman moved back to New Orleans and his wife divorced him and moved to Texas with his children.

Charges were brought and he was convicted of a felony and sent to prison.

While in prison he had a brain aneurism and died. He was forty-six years old.

It is suggested that after each story you _wait_ a moment or so and think about the people you just read about before going on. Thank you.

45 – The Bank

When he entered the branch of the bank, the three tellers were all smiling at him and said, "Good Morning."

It was a very large international bank and it had branches all over the United States. This one was located in a middle class suburb and was recently built from the ground up. It was very modern and impressive.

Miss Osborn was the head teller and she was dressed in a beautiful white blouse and wearing the green blazer with the bank's logo on it. She couldn't be friendlier.

She asked John if he had one of the high interest accounts that the bank had just introduced. He could get higher interest on his savings. It seemed that she really cared in helping him. The fact that she got a bonus for everyone she signed up was not disclosed to John. But he agreed and was introduced to Mary who was the loan officer in the branch.

Mary was also dressed in the bank's green blazer and she too was all teeth when she smiled. Her smile almost went from ear to ear; it was so large and friendly.

It was Mary's job to help with the paperwork and seek out candidates for loans. That was how the bank made their money.

She informed him of their homeowner's equity loans where he could take a mortgage out on his home and he paid a smaller rate of interest. But the interest rate was higher than the new savings rate he had intended to take on the bank account Miss Osborn had told him about.

John was a long-time employee of a small business in town and had worked his way up to be a foreman.

The salary was good and he was able to save a few dollars, and over the years he paid off his house. This homeowner's loan, Mary told him, was just in case he needed extra money.

"The bank cares about you," she said, "and we're just helping you in case there was ever an emergency and you needed the money quickly."

John signed the papers and everyone was very friendly and waved goodbye as he left the bank.

As it turned out the next year he lost his job and he had to pay for his medical insurance himself.

His wife came down with a very serious disease and she had to stop working. Then the great recession hit and John's employer had to close and went out of business.

Luckily he had remembered the homeowner's equity loan he had never used but took out.

He used that money to pay bills with, medications that were not covered by his medical plan, and all his insurance premiums. There were a lot of bills to pay and eventually he used up all the money in the loan account. He couldn't pay them back.

When he went to speak to Mary at the bank she said she couldn't help him. She smiled.

The bank's loan department was located in another state and they were going to start foreclosure proceedings.

It was then that he realized banks are not the friendly people who write the loans and say they care. They just want their interest and if you have to live on the street that's your problem. The faceless loan officers in distant locations thought of John as a loan number, not a person.

They just wanted their interest. John lost everything.

John and his wife were eventually evicted.

Welfare put them in an efficiency motel to live.

It is suggested that after each story you *wait* a moment or so and think about the people you just read about before going on. Thank you.

46 - Life

"Till death do us part," and then he kissed his bride.

That was at the very big wedding they had with almost two hundred and fifty people watching them take their marriage vows.

The band played well into the morning and everyone went home tired but very happy. Bliss.

They fell into a routine that most families fall into. On Saturday nights they went out together. Either they saw a movie, went to the neighborhood bar to shoot pool and hang out with friends, or just went to the local mall to walk around.

At least once a month they went dancing. As a teenage she had wanted to be a professional dancer and she was great at it. When she danced the other people stopped and admired her grace. Her smile lit up the room.

Friday nights they went their own ways. He is with his buddies and her with her two closest girlfriends.

Then one Friday his friends talked him into going to a nightclub. They were drinking and flirting with the girls there. His pals hooked up and went their separate ways. But he didn't go past talking and eventually went home alone.

She came home that night and complained of a pain in her leg. They didn't think much of it and they went to bed.

Very early the next morning she woke up with a severe pain in her leg that actually woke her up. They called an ambulance and went to the hospital emergency room.

At first they thought it was a blood clot. They did some tests and then did more tests. The blood work came back with elevated white blood cells.

The hospital called in a vascular specialist. He thought it was cancer.

That was a good diagnosis.

They prescribed an aggressive course of action after consulting an oncologist.

They treated her with radiation and chemo therapy.

After a while it seemed to work.

She was very tired from everything and had to stop working. She had trouble walking as she was very weak from the treatments.

Then one day they did some more tests and couldn't find any more cancer.

That night she and her husband rejoiced at dinner with the good news.

Hopefully they could start their life together over again. They realized they had a second chance.

She was only in her late twenties. Her long brunette hair was short now but her infectious smile remained. Her outgoing cheerfulness returned and the sun started to shine on them.

After a while she started to walk to regain her stamina.

Her family and friends were there for her every day when she was ill and now they celebrated her recovery. Their prayers had been answered.

Her husband even started to talk about raising a family. But they had to wait for the doctors to okay it. She was still weak but improving.

After a long walk one day she thought she had started to get a cold. She couldn't stop coughing and was very short of breath.

When she coughed up blood her husband drove her to the hospital and her doctors were called in.

They had chest x-rays done.

There was a spot on her lungs.

It was cancer.

They decided to do surgery and remove what they could. When they opened her up on the table they saw it had already spread to the other lung and there was nothing they could do. They closed her up and afterwards told her husband.

She died two weeks after the surgery.

It is suggested that after each story you _wait_ a moment or so and think about the people you just read about before going on. Thank you.

47 - O Called

O called. Well, not really O. One of the producers called.

She read the book I had written and suggested I be a guest on the O show.

My book had just started to take off and Hollywood agents were calling me. They wanted to use some of my short stories as plots for movies.

O then read the book and agreed to have me as a guest.

I accepted and then thought to myself, "What did I get myself into now"?

All of a sudden it hit me. My nerves were rattled, my legs weakened, and I had to sit down. My stomach was in a knot.

Oh my God, I have to lose weight, and really quick. I was scheduled to be on her show in three weeks.

My youngest son has no problem being on television. He works in that medium. He has been performing in comedy clubs in Manhattan and is like a duck to water. He excels when he is "on."

Wait till my wife hears this. And my oldest daughter is crazy about O. She is an O fan going back to when she was in high school.

I remember one day I kept her home from high school during the winter and we went to Sandy Hook National Park with my camera. I pulled onto a parking lot and the temperature had to be in the twenties. There must have been a thousand sea gulls sunning themselves on the concrete. My daughter was afraid to get out. She said it reminded her of a Hitchcock movie. So I had to drive to another lot and we spent the day shooting on the beach. But she had to get back in time to watch O.

After a quick trip to the mall I had everything I needed. Now all I had to do was pack and go talk to O. Almost.

I took along some Xanax. Just in case I needed it.

And Ambien SR.

And the Maalox.

My God, I am packing a small drugstore besides my clothing.

Well the plane ride was great. The car service was there to meet us and whisked us to the hotel we were staying at.

The show was being recorded and I was to be her third guest.

We were taken to the green room (yes it is green to relax nervous Nellies like me) and we were told to just sit and relax.

Sitting with us was a young writer who had written a book on how she went from a lesbian to a bisexual married housewife. It was in the top ten on the *New York Times* book list.

The other writer was a teenager who wrote a book on sexting and how not to get caught.

It was too late for me to take the Xanax. I would fall asleep on the set if I took it now.

I needed nerves of steel.

The producer assigned to me came in and said I was next. Get ready to go on.

Then I remembered what I said to myself when my appendix ruptured and I had to have emergency surgery. I had never been in a hospital as a patient before.

I thought of John Wayne saying, "Damn the torpedoes and full speed ahead."

That's how I coped with my surgery and the O show too.

It is suggested that after each story you *wait* a moment or so and think about the people you just read about before going on. Thank you.

48 - Politics

The congressman left his local office and got into his Lincoln and drove away.

This was his fifth term and things looked good for his re-election to a sixth.

He was pro-choice and favored gay rights legislation. For years that platform had carried the day.

As a Democrat he had voted for President Obama's health plan and a lot of his constituents were mad as heck with him. He was hoping that by the time the election came it would die down.

Also, his girlfriend was pregnant and she lived in Washington near his apartment. He didn't want to leave her and move back north. As long as he was elected things would work themselves out quietly and smoothly.

People don't want to hear that their congressman is fooling around and impregnated a woman who is not his wife. And he didn't want his wife to find out either.

But things looked good for November. He hoped he could ride out the resentment. Otherwise he would be voted out.

The republican candidate was being supported by the new Tea Party and had their backing, both financially and with volunteers.

It seemed like it was going to be a close election and both candidates were prepared for it.

They both had hired political consultants, media people, and were building a large fund of money to carry them through the campaign.

Then things started to get interesting.

The republican candidate was running on family values and found out about his rival's pregnant mistress living in Washington.

Someone in the congressman's office had found out about her and tipped the republicans off to it. Seems this person was slighted by the congressman when she asked for a raise. He was curt with her and her feelings were hurt.

So when she found out about the girlfriend she called the republican's campaign office.

Suddenly the media was full of the scandal. It hit the newspapers, the six o'clock television news and the late night talk shows.

His wife was watching the *Tonight Show* when Jay did a joke about her husband. That's how she found out.

Needless to say it was not a quiet evening at the congressman's home that night.

Meanwhile the President had scheduled a campaign stop during the election season to stump for him one night at a fundraiser. After the news got out the White House called to cancel and said there was a conflict that evening and the president had to honor prior commitments.

It seemed that everything was about to go down in flames.

His wife insisted that the affair be over or she would be divorcing him and cleaning out his bank account. She didn't care how he did it. She was not going to live a different lifestyle than the one she was used to. How he supported the baby was going to be his problem.

The speaking engagements dried up. The book deal he had to put on hold by the publisher until things cleared up. He was writing about inside Washington and how it works. The book was to name names and tell the inside stories that he was part of for ten years.

Then it happened.

The republican's ex-gay lover came forth when he read that his ex was going to fight the gay rights legislation that the democrat supported. He came out of the closet and exposed the candidate as gay, and also bisexual.

Now the republican had a jilted wife to contend with, besides the negative publicity.

This is how American politics works today.

Remember to vote....

It is suggested that after each story you *wait* a moment or so and think about the people you just read about before going on. Thank you.

49 – Aunt Betty

James was a corrections officer at a New York City correctional facility in the 1930s. He was good at what he did and was still single at thirty-one.

They moved him around the jail as they also did with the other guards.

Then one day they brought in a handful of prostitutes to the section where he was working. He spotted a pretty young girl and struck up a conversation with her.

Her name was Betty and she had run away from home and took to the streets to make a living. She was very frail and angelic looking like a small waif that you would imagine in a Dickens novel.

Stringy brown hair cut short above the neck. Her clothes were a little worn and had seen better days. But she had a beautiful smile and James noticed that. He fell in love with her right then and there.

She was only sixteen but told the arresting officers she was eighteen.

When she went to court he took the day off to be there and bailed her out.

When they met outside the courthouse he told her that if she married him he would take care of her for the rest of her life. She wouldn't have to work the streets and he would pay for all her care and things.

She agreed and they were married at city hall the next week.

James had an apartment near Brighton Beach in Brooklyn and they moved in there.

Just as he had said he always took care of her and made sure that whatever she wanted he got her.

During the summers when he went to work she would go to the beach and lay out there all day, near the lifeguard stand.

Naturally the life guards noticed her and sometimes, in the midafternoon if it got too hot, she would invite one of them to her apartment to cool off. But it was always "very hot" when they entered the apartment, in more ways than one.

And the delivery boys who would bring her groceries to the apartment were always given a "special" tip.

James never knew of the guests she brought to the apartment, or at least he never said anything. He was in love with her and didn't want to chance losing her.

This went on for years.

At family functions she was known as Aunt Betty and James' nephews got to know her "very well" also. Once they were sixteen or older she always invited them to go to the beach with her in the summer.

They would go to the beach and then back to her apartment to "cool" off.

As time went by James finally retired and stayed home with Betty. But if he went to the store, or shopping, she always knew who to call for some company.

Then one day James fell ill and died.

Betty was the recipient of his estate and pension.

They never had children but James had treated her as a child his whole life and catered to her whims.

After his death she started to age as she had to do everything herself now.

Wrinkles appeared on her face, and her skin on her arms was dry and wrinkled from the sun, after all those years on the beach.

She had lost her youth and beauty.

But somehow Aunt Betty always found someone to be with her, even though it was for an exceedingly short period of time.

Betty lived this way into her eighties until she died in her apartment alone one night.

It is suggested that after each story you _wait_ a moment or so and think about the people you just read about before going on. Thank you.

50 – Seaside Grove

The sign by the entrance to Seaside Grove said, "NO JEWS, BLACKS, OR DOGS ALLOWED".

Both boys, David who was Jewish and Derik who was black, just stood there looking at the sign. They grew up together and were best friends.

They walked over from a neighboring town to see the Memorial Day Parade and stationed themselves where they thought they would have a good view. It was under some tall trees and the leaves would provide shade from the hot May sun.

But across the street from where they stood were the entrance gates to Seaside Grove and for the first time in their lives they saw that sign.

It was still early and the parade would not start for a while so they did what most curious thirteen years olds would do: they walked across the street, and jumped the fence.

It was easy to find the main street and they started to walk into town looking everywhere to see if they were noticed.

They were noticed and people on their porches stood up with their jaws dropped open.

This had never happened before.

Yes, there were protests in the past, but it was always outside the gates. No one had actually walked into Seaside Grove that wasn't supposed to be there.

The boys were a little nervous because they realized that no one said good morning to them when they walked past. In their town everyone said that if you walked by them. It was the proper thing to do.

As they went further into town, towards the beach, people started to come out of their homes and look at them as they walked on the sidewalk.

When they were in the center of the business district a police car pulled up and stopped next to them.

The officer told them to stop and asked who they were with in town. Upon hearing that they were there by themselves he got out and put them in the backseat of his car. The policeman was on the burly side with many years of experience on a very quiet police force. He probably ate more donuts than he wrote tickets in a year.

The officer said that usually they take people who don't belong there to jail and punish them.

Just the thought of an unknown punishment ripped through the boys minds. All kinds of torture, beatings, and cruelties were imagined as the police car started to drive away.

They started to sweat just thinking of their unknown punishment.

They saw people staring into the backseat of the police car as it drove through town. It went on side streets, in one and then out another, until they had no idea where they were, or were going.

Finally the car drove up to the entry gates and stopped.

The officer opened the rear doors and the boys stepped out and stood there.

They were warned that if they ever entered Seaside Grove again he would not be so kind to them. They would be taken to jail and not heard from again. Their mothers would not know what happened to them, never, ever.

They walked back across the street to where they had originally stood.

The breeze from the ocean blew across their faces and cooled off the sweat dripping from their heads. It was from nerves, not heat.

Music started to play.

They saw the marching bands coming.

Then the soldiers marched right behind them. There were soldiers of all skin colors wearing their Army uniforms.

But some of them couldn't walk in Seaside Grove.

It is suggested that after each story you *wait* a moment or so and think about the people you just read about before going on. Thank you.

51 – The Shop

It was a warm day and he had just picked up the day's cash, almost thirty thousand dollars, from the bank and was driving back to the scrap yard.

They paid out cash for the copper and other non-ferrous metals they bought. He was warm and the driver's side window was open.

He did this every day. It was routine to go to the bank and bring the money back to the scrape yard office.

The car in front of him stopped in the middle of the block and backed up, almost touching his car's bumper. The car behind stopped and blocked him in. Then the drivers of both cars got out, drew guns, put a pistol to his head and handcuffed Abe to the steering wheel and duct-taped his eyes so he could not drive. Then they reached in and took the satchel of cash and drove off.

That was how it all began.

The next day they signed up with an armored car service to deliver the cash to the shop. But that did not stop the thieves.

Two months later they waited in ambush for the armored truck to unload by the shop and they approached with their guns drawn. A gunfight broke out on the street and a security guard lay dead, the money bags taken, and it made the evening news.

This was in broad daylight.

If you went to visit the shop you had to ring a bell, wait for the cameras to scan both sides of where you were standing, and then the steel doors would open and an arm would reach out and pull you inside very quickly.

The safe where the cash was kept was very unique. There were shelves in the bathroom over the toilet. On the shelves were stacks of cash neatly bound in piles waiting to be paid out to their customers.

If you went to use the bathroom you had to use the one upstairs. Only a handful of people were allowed to use that toilet.

Finally they hooked up with the bank and an ATM machine was brought in by the bank and put inside the warehouse. At night a steel gate was drawn down and it was secured.

Now when they bought the scrap metal, the clients were given a slip of paper and they went outside to insert it and get their money.

One day Abe's nephew was called to see if he wanted to buy a lot of scrap copper by the docks. It was to be a cash deal.

He took ten thousand dollars in cash and was walking out the door when Abe asked him where he was going.

He told him about the deal and Abe said not to go. It was a setup. He would never return alive after they robbed him. If they wanted to sell him copper they had to bring it to the shop. There was no other way.

Abe had enough of this nonsense. He spoke to his nephew who grew up with the "boys" in Brooklyn and asked him to make a contact and deal with the holdups.

A call was made and the nephew went with his best friend Anthony to see Anthony's uncle in Howard Beach. The uncle was a capo in a mob family.

After a small conversation explaining the problem the uncle said he could be of help. But Abe would have to hire the uncle's union workers.

The deal was made and they never had another robbery or union problem.

Things just seemed to work themselves out.

It is suggested that after each story you *wait* a moment or so and think about the people you just read about before going on. Thank you.

52 – In-Home Service

"Don't start something you can't finish," she said to him.

He was there to spray her apartment for bugs. He started to make small talk and come on to her.

She was striking, a divorced woman about forty, and was tall and well built. She had a teenage daughter who was at school and this was the woman's day off.

Gary was about her height but gruff looking, with a red plaid shirt, and a day-old beard.

After thinking about it for a minute he kissed her, and then he stopped. He thought better of it. He was afraid he would not be "man" enough for her.

So he got up and finished his job there.

This happened often to him with women. Except he usually didn't back off from a situation like this.

But she was different. She was self-assured and this frightened him.

So he packed up and went to his next stop.

As he parked his service van he couldn't stop thinking about being intimidated by his last call. But it was too late now and he went in to the next apartment.

The young girl was in her mid-twenties and she was home that day while her girlfriend was working.

Gary started to spray the apartment for pests when she started to flirt with him. Before long, one thing led to another and both of them were going at it hot and heavy. This time Gary wasn't backing down.

It didn't matter to him that he was married with two teenage daughters. She was half his wife's age and his ego was being stroked.

The next day they arranged to meet again.

His wife was overweight, worked long hours, and didn't really take the proper care of herself as she should have. She was tired from working two jobs and raising and arguing with her teenage daughters to put much effort into herself. Or put any feelings towards Gary for that matter.

Finally a few weeks later he left his family and moved in with this young girl. The wife was beside herself. She went around the neighborhood talking trash about Gary. She even went to his boss to complain about him but to no avail.

She was hurt and spurned. That is a bad combination and vengeance was now on her mind.

She joined a gym, started to attend weight loss meetings, and took the time to do her hair and nails every week.

Gary sent her money for her and the kids but it was tough to make ends meet. Sometimes he didn't send any money at all.

But she was going to get even.

After six months she was looking really good.

Men were starting to notice her and she was asked out on dates almost every week.

Soon she was dating two men on a steady basis and they were giving her very nice gifts.

One of them proposed marriage to her and she accepted.

But she told him that she had a "problem" and its name was Gary. It turned out he was associated with organized crime and he said he would take care of it for her.

He was a foreman on the docks and he knew the right people to solve the problem.

The Cuban mafia hit men worked cheaply and would just whisk him off the street. Then take him somewhere, torture him, cut him up, and scatter his body parts in the Meadowlands.

After the fish, birds, and rats finished eating the police would never find him.

So one sunny day....

It is suggested that after each story you *wait* a moment or so and think about the people you just read about before going on. Thank you.

53 – Mary the Teller

The first time anyone remembers seeing Mary was her first day on the job. She started as a bank teller in a small local branch in rural New Jersey.

Mary was a local girl who was home schooled and led a sheltered life until she had to go to work at eighteen.

She wore cheap cotton print dresses and had long stringy hair. It was a mousy brown color and she wore no makeup. If you spoke to her she smiled and was friendly but she had that aura of a small town girl.

As a teller she didn't have any problems. Her totals balanced every day and she was never over or under in her monies, which is unusual for a bank teller.

After a while Mary was promoted to assistant head teller. Her branch manager trained her to work the front desk and answer customer questions. She was being groomed to be a head teller.

Mary was sent for additional training so she would be knowledgeable about all the financial products that the bank offered.

This took a few months, on a part-time basis, and finally she was promoted to head teller at her branch office.

She was great at this. No matter what the problem was, she was able to fix it and all the customers were satisfied.

Headquarters started to get letters complimenting her and her name was being mentioned for a promotion.

As head teller her clothes started to get more fashionable

No longer did she wear the printed cotton dresses but business suits from Ann Taylor Loft. Her hair was no longer stringy but coiffed every week in a pleasing style. And she now got her nails professionally polished every week and a pedicure while she was also in the beauty parlor.

Mary never wore jewelry before but now started to sport gold necklaces, gem stone rings, and a bevy of gold bracelets in all the high glamour styles.

She had one beautiful emerald necklace that she would wear on occasion and it was stunning. She told one of the women who was in the bank that she bought it in Atlantic City in one of the casino's jewelry stores.

Now she was no longer the mousy looking local girl but had transformed herself through her hard work into an attractive woman who was being noticed.

Men started to ask her out on dates and she had a very busy social life on the weekends.

She traded in her beat-up old clunker of a car and was seen driving a new red Corvette convertible.

All financial dealings in the branch were done through Mary as she was the only one there that really understood what the complicated transactions were. She was that good.

The district managers were talking to her about going for training as a branch manager as she was really doing that job already. She picked it up on the fly. Also she started to read the manuals in her spare time and was self-taught.

Everything was going great until a customer came in and wanted to cash in his two-year certificate of deposit (CD). He had the certificate in his hand but the teller couldn't find any trace of it in the bank's computers.

It seemed that if someone wanted a long-term CD Mary printed the certificate for them and kept the cash!

The bank examiners figured she took almost half a million dollars and gambled most it away in the casinos.

She now has free room and board for a minimum of twenty years.

It is suggested that after each story you *wait* a moment or so and think about the people you just read about before going on. Thank you.

54 – Life in Ancient Israel

When Moishe was thirteen he was a bar mitzvah, at eighteen he was put into an arranged marriage, and then he started to procreate like the stars in the heavens. Baby after baby was born into his family.

One day he was taking the garbage out because it smelled with the baby's poopy papyrus diapers.

He was holding his nose and didn't see a Babylonian sneak up behind him and klop him on the head.

Moishe was taken as a slave and forced to schlep to Babylon by foot to work with the other thousands of slaves they had captured.

But there was a problem. Too many slaves and not enough work.

So Moishe sat around with the other boychicks and all they did was schmooze and talk about the good old days.

Then one evening someone decided they should use their spare time (that was all they had anyway) constructively and start to write.

They spent a few days deciding what to write when one fellow said, "Why not write down the entire dos and don'ts that we know from when we were in Israel?"

They divided up into groups and started to talk and write all their rules down.

Moishe was in the group with Yaakov, Dovey, and Schlomo.

So one day while writing Moishe felt very sour. He wondered how he got into this pickle of a situation in Babylon.

He remembered he was taking out the smelly garbage when he was hit on the head and made to walk a thousand miles to Babylon and become a slave.

So that day he snuck out to continue the tractate he was writing that Jewish husbands were prohibited from taking the garbage out from Sunday through Friday. They could only take it out on Saturday, unless they were in synagogue praying and partaking in the Oneg [lunch].

He told this to the other guys in his group and they all agreed. So they raised their cups of sweet swill (Manishewitz kosher wine wasn't invented yet) and toasted the inclusion into the Talmud (the do's and don'ts) what Moishe had written.

But as luck would have it, one night a Rabbi named Rashi was editing the Talmud by candlelight.

He was dipping his day-old bread into olive oil when a few drops of oil fell onto the page where Moishe had written about taking out the garbage.

Not being able to read it, Rashi discarded that portion, and it never made it into the final version of the Talmud that is used today.

But the concept was not lost.

All the guys in Moishe's group remembered what he wrote and they told their sons about it.

It was passed down by word of mouth from father to son for thousands of years.

Every generation remembered it.

And to this day not one Jewish husband will take out the garbage no matter how high it is piled in the kitchen.

His wife has to command him to take it out or do it herself.

It all goes back to life in ancient Israel.

It is suggested that after each story you *wait* a moment or so and think about the people you just read about before going on. Thank you.

55 – Karla

Slowly she slid the knife out of its sheath as he turned over with his back to her.

They were just lying down on a purple striped blanket with gold stars on it that she always kept in her car. But the scrub brush was very irritating so they had to move further down the ravine where it had a flatter surface.

There was no one around for miles. They were in the woods at an old abandoned iron mine in rural New Jersey. It was used as an unofficial dump by people who had to get rid of stuff and didn't want anyone to find it, or see them.

Karla had just met him in a bar earlier that evening and they hit it off. He believed that she was easy so they left and she drove him to this spot.

She was just over five feet tall, had short brown hair, and skinny. Almost anorexic, but not quite.

Her parents died when she was a teenager and she went through a series of disastrous relationships that drastically affected her mentally.

This evening the guy she picked up in a bar was named Sid and he was looking for a good time.

He turned back to face her. She suggested they tie each other up and quickly tied his hands together, then his legs. Without saying a word he was dead very quickly.

This was not the first time it happened. Sid was just another revenge killing for all the men who took advantage of Karla and left her almost broke.

She felt no remorse.

It was a few weeks before someone discovered the body.

The police now realized they had a serial killer on their hands as she always tied up her victims and knifed them to death. The killings made the news shows and Karla was aware of this. Karla took their wallets and jewelry to make it look like a robbery. Karla pawned the jewelry and that paid for breast enhancement surgery.

She started to wear a long blonde wig when she went out and now used makeup to change her appearance. Eventually her hair grew in and she had it bleached strawberry blonde.

There was one detective, Jay Hines, who was determined to catch the killer. He knew they were looking for a woman but no one could accurately describe her other than her being thin, brunette, and on the petite side.

Jay started to hang out in bars at night in the Dover area. It seems most of the men were from Sussex County. He concentrated his efforts there.

But it didn't help. He was up against a dead end and he was very frustrated. All he could hope for was that the killer would make a mistake and leave some clues to solve the case. Or that someone would see something, hear of the murder, and report it.

So in July he took his vacation in Belmar on the Jersey shore. He was single, in his early thirties, and available.

He stayed at a nearby bed and breakfast and was able to walk a few blocks to the beach.

The first day he went to the beach and sat under a beach umbrella enjoying the gentle breeze coming off the ocean. He glanced over and saw some girls sitting nearby. He noticed one and she smiled at him.

He was entranced and went over to talk to her. She was lying on a purple striped blanket with gold stars on it....

It is suggested that after each story you *wait* a moment or so and think about the people you just read about before going on. Thank you.

56 - Lebanon

Abdul-Azim was sitting with men in southern Lebanon discussing their next attack. He had been trained in Iran and was here to lead them in battle.

They were talking well into the early evening when one of them asked if they could have some hot tea.

Mohammad got up and went over to the portable propane stove, placed the teapot on the burner, and lit the stove.

It exploded, sending shrapnel all over the small room and killing everyone in it.

Hezbollah couldn't understand why it happened. How could a propane stove explode like that? There must have been a leak in the line, they thought. Or maybe an Israeli bomb somehow made it into the bunker.

Six months earlier when Abdul-Azim got back from Iran, he was in a café in Beirut when the waitress came over to take his order.

She started to talk to him and she said it was terrible what the Israelis had done to their country. Her brother and father were killed in the recent invasion and she would do anything to settle the score.

He liked what he heard and thought that she would be useful in the future.

What she didn't tell him was that she was a Lebanese Christian and that Hezbollah had killed her family members with their indiscriminate shelling. She was out to get revenge and was working for Mossad.

Abdul spoke to her about how he was going to train men to get back at Israel.

He was going to bring weapons into Lebanon through Syria over the mountain passes. He was told where to go and who to ask for when the Syrian military stopped him. Everything was preplanned for him by the Iranian secret police.

All he had to do was get a few men to transport the weapons by truck into the south and the rest would be easy.

He thought that if this woman traveled with them it would not arouse much suspicion. It was unusual for a woman to be involved in weapons smuggling and they would let him pass without a thorough inspection.

It seemed to work and they reached their goal with the weapons.

Once they settled in, she prepared dinner for the men, served it, and washed the dishes.

The next evening they started to unload the trucks after dusk while she cleaned up.

Carefully she placed the C4 under the stove, attached the two detonating cord clips, and ran the wire to a cell phone in a box that she buried with the explosives under the stove.

The stove was in the corner and there was no way anyone could step on the package, even if they moved the stove.

She wasn't sure what excuse she could use to get out of there so she could set it off. But she was lucky.

When the trucks were unloaded the men came in and told her to leave them alone for a while. They had business to discuss and sent her outside.

She walked out and was met by a guard. He started to talk to her and she realized her time was limited. She had to get away and make the call to set off the bomb.

But he insisted on talking to her.

Time was running out. They would leave soon.

She said she had to go to the bathroom and she started to walk back in.

Before she entered she took out her cell phone and dialed it.

She was close, too close, some would think, when the bomb went off....

It is suggested that after each story you *wait* a moment or so and think about the people you just read about before going on. Thank you.

57 - Todd

Todd was an unloved son.

In all his sixteen years, he never heard someone tell him he was loved, or even wanted.

His parents were very wealthy and had a slew of nannies raise him until he was five. Then he was sent away to boarding school for his education and upbringing.

The education was first-rate and the resident attendant was an older lady who took a liking to him. She was very kind to him and would always listen to him and help out any way she could. In many ways she was a surrogate mother to Todd.

There was a dance at a girl's boarding school nearby and the staff at the school arranged for it to take place one Saturday evening.

At the dance Todd met Ivy who was very attractive and had a lively personality. She had long black hair that contrasted nicely with her olive skin. Being of Hispanic ancestry she had a beautiful Latina aura about her.

Todd on the other hand was tall, blond, blue eyes, and very Caucasian.

Ivy was there on a scholarship from a foundation. She came from an urban school district and they sent two students a year to this upper class school for an education.

She was very bright, but on the wild side.

They decided to sneak out of the dance and go outside behind some bushes.

She showed him some affection.

Stroked his hair, held him tightly, and kissed him ever so gently on the lips.

He was smitten with her and for the first time he felt something towards another human being that he never experienced before.

But that was all that happened. They didn't go any further, sexually, than kissing.

Ivy had a secret, but now was not the time to let it out. She wanted to make sure that Todd was serious before she told him, or anyone else. No one at school knew and she wanted to keep it that way.

Todd's friends at school at first were envious of him. She was very striking and the life of the party when they all got together socially.

But Todd never got beyond kissing. He thought that maybe she had something in her past that stopped her from going further.

He didn't know what it was. She was so outgoing and vibrant, and easy to kiss. But that's where she stopped.

His classmate thought it was unusual that in today's "anything goes" climate, a young inner city girl didn't go all the way.

Ivy told him that one day he would find out, but not yet.

They had to be older and a commitment had to be made before she let her secret be known.

The year passed very quickly and they were still going out with each other.

He respected her wishes and was deeply in love with her. She was the only one in his life that ever hugged him or showed emotions to him.

They graduated and decided to go to college together.

Only a state school with a dormitory was where she could afford to go, and he decided to join her there.

In their junior year of college he had decided that he wanted to marry Ivy.

He went out and bought an engagement ring for Ivy.

That night they went out for dinner and he proposed to her.

She told him that she cannot have children. He didn't care.

Then she told him her secret. She was a hermaphrodite.

Todd was dumbfounded. He stood up…and walked away.

Ivy ran after him….

It is suggested that after each story you *wait* a moment or so and think about the people you just read about before going on. Thank you.

58 - Voices

"Yes, your honor, I killed him".

"I shot him in the chest and didn't stop until I ran out of bullets" Peter said out loud so everyone in the courtroom could hear him.

When asked why he did it he responded that he heard voices in his head and they didn't stop until the victim died.

The judge said that he accepted the plea deal and that Peter would serve life without parole in prison.

On the ride upstate to the prison he started to hear the voices again. They told him he would escape and the voices would help him.

Peter was confused. He didn't want to kill anybody, or even escape. But these voices somehow compelled him to act against his nature and personality.

Once in the prison gates the van stopped. Peter and the other handful of men got out of the van and stood there looking at the thirty foot high gray stone walls.

The voice told Peter that the next day he would be escaping. He shut his eyes and was confused. The voices were back. Somehow they were always right and when they told him things, it happened.

The next day he was in the prison orientation room where the new inmates were introduced to the staff sergeant and the rules of the institution were told to them once. If they didn't understand them then they would learn the hard way.

That afternoon Peter was led into the prison exercise yard. He walked around it very calmly. Glancing at the guard towers he saw officers with rifles looking down into the yard.

He had no idea how he would escape but the voices in his head were always right.

Then he heard the voices tell him to go to the southern wall of the prison yard. There he saw repair work being done to the wall. There was a cement mixer and a lift to bring the men up to the top of the wall so they could make repairs.

"Now" the voice yelled into his head.

He ran to the lift, hoped in, and started to make the bucket go to the top of the wall.

No one noticed. He was amazed.

Once on top he took his jacket off, wrapped it around the barbed wire for protection, and used the wire to lower himself off the wall to the ground below.

He started to run when he heard the sirens going off.

It was midafternoon and he saw a small wooded area ahead and he ran for it to hide.

He was sweating profusely. He knew that they would be out with dogs tracking his scent.

He bolted further into the woods until he came to a dirt road.

Peter quickly followed it as it wound its way up into the mountains.

The dogs were barking but they started to fall further away from the direction he was going.

As Peter turned a corner he ran right into two state troopers with their guns pointed directly at him.

His heart was beating so fast it felt like it would burst out of his chest.

Peter had to make a decision.

Then he heard the voice again....

"What do you think we should do with Peter now" said Tim.

The two boys sitting at the computer were getting tired of the reality game.

They set it on auto-play and went for lunch.

"Peter, that's a great game you just programmed" said the supervisor. "How creative, a game within a game".

"Which is the reality?" he said before lunch.

It is suggested that after each story you *wait* a moment or so and think about the people you just read about before going on. Thank you.

59 - A Final Goodbye

She was lying there motionless on her death bed. The oxygen was being pumped through a tube into her nostrils, and the saline drip was going in through her right forearm.

It was the end of a life as a mother, wife, sister and a loving daughter.

Lee was the embodiment of what a good person should be.

She raised five children, worked a full time job, took care of a household, and was a faithful wife.

Yet here she was dying of cancer.

Twenty years before she had her first cancer operation and it was successful.

But the chemo she took afterwards took its toll on her body. Yet she pushed herself to go to work every day. That was her therapy that kept her going.

This time the cancer spread too far, and she refused to have chemo again. She felt it was time.

Previously when she had chemo she would come home from work, cook dinner, and help the kids with their homework.

The she would go to bed and rest until the next morning.

Her husband usually came home late from work and would clean up and eat his meals with whatever kids didn't finish earlier. He never woke her or bothered her once she went to bed.

When her older sister had serious surgery and couldn't live alone she took her in and she stayed for over a year with Lee's family.

Never did she complain.

When Lee reached sixty she wanted to retire but her husband lost his business and she had to continue working. She supported the family when her husband couldn't.

Years before she was there the time her youngest daughter stole her car and went on a heroin induced crime spree across three states with her boyfriend.

Lee spent half her salary that year paying for long term drug rehabilitation for her daughter to get clean and start a new life. She also paid for a lawyer to keep her daughter out of prison. Although she did keep her in the country jail until there was an opening in the program. That was for four months but she knew better than to let her out. Tough love worked.

Yet here she was asleep from the pain killing drugs. She was not conscious and did not know who was with her.

Her husband of fifty five years came in the room and sat down beside her. Gently her took her hand and stroked it softly.

He always thought they would retire together and enjoy their last years in a sunny place. Maybe Florida, maybe the southwest, but it was not going to happen now.

Carefully her pushed her hair away from her face and ever so lightly pressed his hand on her cheek.

He was devastated. He was losing his life partner and his best friend.

They went everywhere together, except for one week every summer. That week she went to the Jersey shore with her sister. They always stayed in Cape May in a motel with an ocean front porch.

That was the only time they were inseparable.

Her children and grandchildren all came in to see her for one last time.

They remembered how she took care of her mother when she was dying of cancer. Every day she went there and did what she could.

When her father became ill and could not live alone she took him in to her house and cared for him until he became bedridden.

Lee opened her eyes one last time, saw her cherished family, smiled and took her last breath.

It is suggested that after each story you _wait_ a moment or so and think about the people you just read about before going on. Thank you.

60 - NASA

Historically India has stories about Vimana's. They are flying machines thought to have existed thousands of years ago in India.

Darleen Johnson is an engineer with NASA in Texas and she read about these machines and started to build one in her barn.

It took years of experimentation dealing with mercury as a metal, and gyroscopes, to make and conduct electricity.

She was helped by her friend Susan who also worked at NASA. They were both in their late thirties and had been in the astronaut training program.

But the space exploration program was not refunded.

So in their spare time they read, studied, saved, and bought what they could to build a Vimana, or space craft, based as closely to the legend as they could.

They found that even in the mountains of Mexico there were stories of men from space that visited Earth. The carvings on ancient temples told the story.

The Asian Indian legends go back almost six thousand years. The men that flew the Vimana's wore bright metallic clothes similar to what our astronauts wear today.

Both women kept up their gym routines from when they were in astronaut training, but not every day. They were still buff, though.

The machine they were building resembled a roundish plane with wings. It was not too big and almost filled the one hundred year old barn.

Government surplus was purchased whenever they thought an item might be useful. They improvised when they had to but this was a real scientific undertaking.

No one knew about it. They felt they would be ridiculed if word got out.

Finally they were finished.

They brought chain saws and cut away a very large part of the barn so they could tow it out into the open field.

Their theory was that the gyroscopes would produce enough electricity, with a magnetic field, combined with the mercury alloys, to lift it up.

They had bought an oxygen replacement device from NASA surplus and were hoping they would not need a space suit. They couldn't get their hands on one anyway.

Carefully they opened the hatch and climbed in. They strapped themselves into the form fitting flight chairs, started the engines, and were hoping for the best.

Slowly they gave the gyroscopes more power. The magnetic field was stable around them.

They started to reverse the field, ever so slightly. The craft started to rise in the air. By adjusting the field they could move forwards, backwards, or go straight up.

They were having a ball with it. They decided to go as high as they could and then open it up to see how fast it would go.

In an instant they were miles above the earth. They slowed down and stabilized the magnetic field so they just hovered above the earth.

The decided to reverse the gyroscopes field against the Earth's magnetic field and pull themselves into the moons magnetic field.

As the craft rose further into the air it started to vibrate. Bolts that were tight were loosening; screws were turning and falling out. Smoke was coming from the mercury holding tanks and seeping into the craft.

A small rumble was heard coming from the gyroscope and they were starting to descend rapidly.

Sweat was beading on their brows as they calmly but quickly tried to land the craft safely.

They had proven their theory that people could travel in space but it might be too late for anyone to ever hear about it.

There was too much smoke in the cabin, their breathing was labored, and they heard a snapping sound as they were coming down to the ground.

The craft was accelerating now as it hurtled towards earth.

They looked at each other, and then….

It is suggested that after each story you *wait* a moment or so and think about the people you just read about before going on. Thank you.

61 – The Date

This could have been called the blind date from Hell.

It started innocently enough with an ad on an online dating service. Harris saw her picture and liked what he read about her on her profile. So he emailed her.

They emailed back and forth a few times then spoke on the phone. This went on for a week or so and finally a date was arranged.

She lived in Manhattan and he was from New Jersey.

He drove into Manhattan and was to meet her at an arranged public location.

It was on the Upper East Side and he parked and walked a few blocks to greet her.

Harris's brother had lived on East 83 Street and Third Avenue. He had found a great bar/restaurant in the neighborhood. It was very tiny, with a bar in front. If you looked in you only saw a small bar. But in the rear was a fantastic restaurant. If you walked by and looked in you would never go in. But the food was gourmet and tasted unbelievably good. And for Manhattan the prices were reasonable.

So Harris was going to take her there for dinner. He had eaten there many times with his family when they visited his brother and enjoyed the food.

As they approached the place they noticed that it was closed. There was a sign from the city board of health that they were closed for rat infestation.

"And this was where you wanted to eat?" she said to him. "I know a good sushi restaurant very close to here. Let's go there, okay?" she asked. Harris thought that he could always order chicken because he didn't eat sushi. So he agreed to go there.

It was a small sushi restaurant. Their table was in the middle of the place and if you stretched your arm you would touch another table. They were packed very tightly as is the custom in Manhattan restaurants.

They ordered and their meals arrived.

She was going to teach him how to eat with chop sticks.

He held them in his hands and started to pick up a piece of his chicken and bring it up to his mouth. But as he raised his arm it slipped out of the chop sticks and in slow motion he saw it tumble into the soy sauce and splatter on her blouse.

Without thinking he immediately grabbed his napkin and started to blot the stains on her blouse. She asked him to please stop doing that as he was patting her breasts without realizing it.

He offered to pay for the cleaning or buy her another blouse.

When things settled down they started to eat.

She asked him to try her sushi and quickly put a piece of sushi into his mouth before he could decline it.

He started to gag.

Quickly he spit it out into his napkin.

He grabbed the sides of the table and started to dry heave until his six foot body shook. The extremely loud gagging sounds, and his violent heaving, startled the other diners and they all stopped eating and looked at him.

This went on for about a minute or longer.

He could not control his gag reflex. He was sweating profusely at this point and finally he was able to stop and sit back in his chair exhausted.

Then his cell phone rang.

It was his date.

She was standing on the corner outside. She said she was never so embarrassed in her life and she was going home by herself.

It is suggested that after each story you *wait* a moment or so and think about the people you just read about before going on. Thank you.

62 - High School

High School was great, maybe.

It was the early 1960's and rock and roll was being established. Fast cars, bikinis, and adolescence were in full bloom.

The universal quest by hormone raging teens, both male and female, was no different than it was before, or after.

Michael's neighbor across the street was a small Jewish doctor, barely five foot tall. He was elderly and married to a tall (over six foot) German woman who used to walk her dachshund in her flowing nightgowns on the street.

She once told him and his friend that girls want to meet boys as badly as boys want to. That struck a chord with him and he never forgot it.

It was Michael's first year in high school and gym was a required class. Who wants to run around and get sweaty at eleven in the morning and go through the rest of the day smelling? So most of the guys just sat around and talked while the jocks played basketball or worked out.

Then one day when the class was over and they were back in the locker room changing, one of the senior boys brought some girls into the locker room. He remembers the stir, and the girls laughing and looking. Brooklyn was a fun place to grow up.

There were so many girls and he was so young.

Wendy was in his homeroom class. She was a tall Irish girl and he had an irresistible crush on her. But she dated older boys and he knew he had no chance with her. But that crush lasted throughout high school. It got no further than good morning.

Then there was the bookkeeping class he took in his senior year because his father thought it wouldn't hurt to know what business was about.

There he saw Francesca for the first time. She looked like a young Mary Tyler Moore when she wore her hair in a flip like the star did.

She was cute, very outgoing, and he wanted to ask her out. He really liked her. Then one day she came over to him and said he knew her boyfriend. Oh no, he was his big brother in the fraternity. He could never ask her out now.

Many years later he met her when she came into a place of business where he was working. She was now divorced with children.

Michael told her that he was crazy about her and had wanted to ask her out in high school. She then asked me why he didn't. He told her she wouldn't have gone out with him as she was in love with her then boyfriend, now ex-husband.

She looked at him, realized he said the truth, and didn't respond. Michael was now married and didn't say anything else to her.

There were others too numerous to name.

One he had dated made it into the grand finals of the Miss Teenage Beauty contest. She was very pretty (a little narcissist), and lived in New Jersey. He didn't drive then. He was only sixteen so she became a summer romance. But he enjoyed her company and liked going out with her.

Then there were his sister's friends.

Once he asked one of her friends to go steady with him. She was very pretty, great personality, and well built. It mattered to her that he never even took her out on a date.

But that was in high school for him. Michael just dove right in.

It is suggested that after each story you _wait_ a moment or so and think about the people you just read about before going on. Thank you.

63 - Cheryl

"I can't believe what a bitch you are being right now" Cheryl sobbed to her latest love as she packed her belongings to leave.

They were together for almost nine months and things were going great until last night.

"It was only a hello kiss, it meant nothing. Why are you breaking up over this? I knew Kathy years ago and haven't seen her for ages. Come on Sue, you know I love you."

Cheryl was upset, but a controlled upset. In reality she knew that what she did was wrong, and it was more than a simple hello kiss. She had passionately kissed Kathy and held her tightly. Although she had played Kathy she still had strong feelings for her, even though she was involved with Sue.

Cheryl was a player. Tall, slim, with short pixie cut hair she liked to play the field. Sue on the other hand was short with long flowing blond hair. She was very feminine and her blue eyes sparkled when she smiled.

Cheryl was smitten by her looks and personality and had made a commitment to her. But last night she broke that vow, ever so slightly. But it was enough for Sue to decide to leave. She was not going to be a third wheel or someone else's standby hookup. She wanted to love and be loved, in full, in return.

When Sue finally left the apartment Cheryl sat down on her sofa and stared at the walls. She was never the one to be left; she was the one who always did the leaving.

Now she knew what a broken heart felt like.

Since college she had been exclusively with girls. Her college roommate had introduced, or discovered, that she had a secret desire for her. She didn't understand it at first. Her feelings were unknown to her. She had grown up dating boys in high school and was a cheerleader.

After a practice when the girls would go to the showers she had this strange compulsion to look at them. There was this one girl that caught her eye. But Cheryl did nothing forward. She just stared at her, and was self-conscious doing so. She didn't comprehend her feelings then, now she did, and she acted on them often.

But this was a first for her. She actually felt bad that it ended with Sue.

It was a few weeks later and she received a phone call from Kathy that she wanted to have lunch with her. Kathy wanted to tell her something.

Cheryl's heart started to beat faster. She was excited that her old love might be back in her life.

Kathy was an average sized girl, a little on the chubby side, but pretty and had been very hurt when Cheryl walked out on her.

She knew Cheryl was a player but could not resist being with her. She gambled on love and eventually lost. She was devastated when Cheryl dumped her.

But lunch could be the beginning of something again, Cheryl thought.

They would meet in Greenwich Village at a small café they used to go to when they were together. She believed this was a good sign.

She was smiling and looking for Kathy.

Sitting at "their" table was Kathy drinking a coffee. Her pink blouse and skirt stood out against the dark walls of the café.

"Cheryl, I wanted to tell you something" Kathy said. "I met someone and am in a relationship with her. You know her. It's Sue".

Kathy learned quickly. Revenge was sweet.

The player was played.

It is suggested that after each story you _wait_ a moment or so and think about the people you just read about before going on. Thank you.

64 – The Will

Mary didn't trust her.

It was taking too long and she wasn't getting any information from the lawyer that was handling the will.

Their mother had died and he made Betty the executrix of his estate. It wasn't a very large estate but he knew that Betty would take care of everything.

The mother had told Betty, who was the older sibling that she had to take care of her sister. But he neglected to say the same thing to Mary.

Betty had a small business in Chicago and was very bright and a caring person.

Her success enabled her to be active in many charities. She gave of her time and money to make things happen when people were in need. Not many people knew what she did.

There was the family that lost their house to black mold and had to move out. Betty made arrangements for them to have a free apartment until they reestablished themselves.

In business she had a soft spot for the underprivileged. She had on at least four occasions hired ex-convicts. One was a mass murderer (2 men in a bar fight), one spent ten years in prison for attempted murder (it was a street fight when he was twenty one), the third was arrested in Florida for something he never found out what, and the fourth was convicted of burglary.

They were all loyal employees through the years and were grateful for the opportunity she gave them to improve their lives.

But her sister had problems.

She tried teaching, and then other jobs, mainly part time. Mary was trying to find something she liked.

The fact that her husband was a CPA and supported them both enabled Mary to stay home for long periods of time trying to "find" herself. Or at the very least a job that she liked and was not too stressful. After all, she didn't have to work.

So when their mother died and Mary was talking to her friends she started to wonder if Betty was trying to steal money from the estate. She did not receive any paperwork from the lawyer or her sister. Mary started to wonder what was going on.

So one day she called her sister and asked where the papers are. Her girlfriends all got reams of paperwork when their parents died, why she wasn't getting any.

Betty calmly told her that the lawyer said he had six months to decide how to value the stock portfolio that their father had left. It could be valued either at the amount when he died or the value six months later. That was why the delay.

Two weeks later Betty received a letter from an attorney stating that he was retained by her sister to "oversee" the execution of the will and its terms.

Betty was devastated. The only person her mother told her she could trust for the rest of her life now thought she was stealing, and she wasn't.

She called her lawyer who was handling the estate and asked to be relieved and have her sister handle it alone.

The lawyer said that he didn't think it was a good idea. She might not do things properly as she lived in California thousands of miles away.

So Betty remained as executrix and called her brother-in-law at his place of business. She said she would never speak to her sister again. She was dead as far as she was concerned. Betty no longer had a sister.

Eventually things got smoothed over and they spoke.

But after many years, the hurt never left.

It is suggested that after each story you _wait_ a moment or so and think about the people you just read about before going on. Thank you.

65 - Blanche I

In the late 1800s in Polish Russia in the back room of a two-room wooden clapboard house, a young woman was giving birth to her first child. She was only in her late teens, but that was the custom in the Orthodox Jewish community.

Men would study Torah and Talmud and girls would be married off at an early age.

Some were married as early as fourteen if it was an arranged marriage. It usually was arranged and a dowry had to be paid.

The midwife was there, as was an older married friend of the mother-to-be. Her parents were dead many years and she lived with her husband.

It was a quiet evening and her husband had gone to evening prayers. Suddenly horsemen rode out from the forest road and into the small village. They had their swords and guns drawn and started to kill whoever was on the streets. It was a slaughter as the Jews in this town were peaceful and unarmed. It was a pogrom and the aim was to kill as many Jews as possible.

The Cossacks showed no mercy. Men, women, and children were brutally slaughtered. They were slashed with the horsemen's swords, or shot, or the small children were run over by the horses.

Her husband was walking to synagogue and he was cut down and killed.

At that same time the mayhem was going on outside the mother-to-be delivered a very tiny baby girl. But she then started to hemorrhage. There was no doctor in the village and the midwife tried everything she knew to stop the bleeding. But nothing helped and she died shortly after giving birth. The mother had wanted to name her Blanche, so that was the name she was given.

As she grew up she was shuttled from one home to another as there were no living relatives that could afford to raise her by themselves. The Jews in the village were very poor and always helped one another out of necessity.

Blanche used to clean their homes to help repay their kindness.

She would wear hand-me-down shoes stuffed with straw in the winter to insulate them and also to cover the holes in the soles. When it got really cold she would walk along the railroad tracks picking up coal that dropped off from the train engines in order to help heat the home she was living in.

Being under five feet tall and very petite, she was easy to dress with others people's old clothes. Everything looked baggy on her as she was so small.

One day a man came to the house where she was living. He had a ticket for his niece to go to America but she was very ill and the ticket would go to waste if it was not used. So the community paid him for the ticket and decided to send Blanche to America on the steamship.

Blanche was only fifteen at the time and she really had no choice but to go. She had a hard life in the village and it couldn't have been any worse in America.

One of the elderly women went with her to the ship to see her off.

Just before Blanche walked up the gangplank to enter the ship she paused and turned to the elderly woman who took her there.

"What was my mother's name she asked?"

"Laura," was the answer.

It is suggested that after each story you _wait_ a moment or so and think about the people you just read about before going on. Thank you.

66 - Blanch II

As the ship entered New York Harbor Blanch looked out in amazement at the buildings. She had never seen such a sight in her life. Growing up in rural Poland, this was like being sent to another planet. She could not comprehend what she was looking at.

Before she left the woman told her that someone would meet her in America and get her a place to stay and a job. All she knew was cleaning houses. Girls in rural Jewish villages were not sent to school, only the boys were. She could read Yiddish as the women in her village taught her, and only enough Polish so she would not get lost. But Yiddish was her first language.

When it was time for her to leave Ellis Island a woman came to take her to a housekeepers job in the Bronx. There she would clean, keep the house, and act as a nanny for the young children.

Everyday Blanch would take the younger children to a park to pay. While there she would meet and talk to the other nannies. She was learning English from them, and from the children she cared for.

Her employers were a young Jewish family that lived in a big house near the Grand Concourse.

The husband was a good looking man in his late thirties and he took a liking to her.

Blanch was only sixteen and had started to develop as young girls do. She had feelings, urges that were new to her. Finally the husband visited her in her room one night.

Two months later she discovered she was pregnant.

The husband told his wife that Blanch had dated a scoundrel and abandoned her. They would keep her employed until the baby was born but after that she would have to find other accommodations. It would be too much to take care of her newborn and their children at the same time.

So after the birth of her daughter another nanny told her of a widow in New Jersey who needed help.

Arrangements were made and Blanch moved to a one room boarding house New Jersey with her daughter.

The widower was a butcher with 8 children. Blanch was now twenty and the oldest child was a son seventeen. But Blanch forged ahead and worked in the butcher shop and took care of the children as if they were her own. She took her daughter with her every day and both went back to their one room at night.

The butcher was twenty five years her senior and was grateful for her help.

One day one of the butcher's sisters was talking to Blanch and suggested that they get married. He needed a wife and Blanch a home for her daughter.

So the arrangement was made and they married.

Blanch was a hard worker and helped in the shop every day. She cooked for the family, cleaned the house, and cared for the children. They aged eight to seventeen. She became their mother and loved them as if they were her own.

The younger children responded and called her mother or mom. There was genuine affection.

A few years passed and the butcher had a stroke and could not work.

It fell on Blanche's shoulders to work the butcher shop alone. She now had the additional duties of also caring for an invalid husband while still maintaining the household.

She did this and never complained.

Blanch was about five feet tall and was lugging sides of beef every day in the shop.

But she kept the family together and surviving.

It is suggested that after each story you *wait* a moment or so and think about the people you just read about before going on. Thank you.

67 – Blanch III

The years past and Blanch was working as hard as a father, mother, and butcher, all rolled into one person.

World War one was raging in Europe and the oldest son was in the army there. He would write letters home to her that almost read like love letters instead of a son to his mother. They were only a year apart in age, but never took that other step.

The youngest adopted daughter, Henrietta, ran off and married a young Italian boy name Gino. Blanch had practically raised her since she was eight years old.

Blanche's husband, still an invalid, forbid his daughter's name be mentioned. She married outside the faith and he sat in morning for her. She was dead to him and his family.

Blanch had heard that Henrietta had moved to Hoboken and had a baby daughter.

So one day she took her infant baby with her and took a bus to Hoboken to search for Henrietta. She barely spoke English but was determined to find her stepdaughter.

She went door to door asking if anyone knew a Jewish girl married to a boy named Gino. People passing on the street were asked, strange doors were knocked on, but no one knew who she was asking for.

Then she knocked on a door in a row house and the woman who answered said she never heard of them. Discouraged, but not giving up, she turned around and started to walk away. From a window on the third floor Henrietta had just looked out by chance, saw Blanch, and called out to her.

She helped her up the stairs and they had a nice reunion. Blanch had brought meat from the butcher shop for her in case she needed it. She didn't tell her husband the butcher.

Now that she knew where she lived she came every week by bus to help out for an afternoon. Gino remembered her kindness. Forty years later when Blanch was in need of a glaucoma operation and she didn't have insurance, Gino paid for the operation.

The butcher shop was being run by Blanch until one day two men came in to see her.

One of the boys had run up big gambling debts and if she didn't pay them off they were going to kill him.

At this time she was now a widow and most of the kids had moved out. But she was still caring for five children, including her own daughter.

Blanch had to sell the butcher shop to pay off the debt. Unfortunately she lived in the apartment upstairs over the shop and she now had to move out. She had a little money left over and had to look for rooms for the family to live in.

No one wanted to rent to a family with that many children.

One day she went to rent rooms and the land lady, Mrs. DiGennaro, took her in because she had only her daughter with her. She failed to mention the other four children.

So one by one they would sneak into the apartment after they moved in.

Finally Mrs. DiGennaro noticed that there were many children coming and going and she asked Blanch, who she called Mrs. Schmidt, how many kids does she rally have?

Mrs. DiGennaro and Mrs. Schmidt were about the same age.

She took pity on her and since they had been living there for six months already, and did no damage or made no noise, she let them stay.

For the rest of their lives they remained friends.

And they always addressed each other as Mrs. Schmidt and Mrs. DiGennaro.

It is suggested that after each story you *wait* a moment or so and think about the people you just read about before going on. Thank you.

68 – The Last Kiss

She was in her early twenties and arrangements were made to have Bessie travel from Polish Austria to America to get married. It was an arranged marriage.

She was educated at home by tutors. That was how her mother was taught. Girls were usually not educated in Eastern Europe at that time.

Bessie arrived in America and what happened next is not known. But the marriage was called off.

She was stranded and alone. A charity helped to settle her in and find work for her.

Bessie was very upset as she was hoping to bring over her sisters Ethie and Frances. Also her young brother Julian was in an orphanage and she wanted him too. But her plans collapsed when the marriage did not take place. Her fiancé had reneged about bringing her family over.

On the rebound she was introduced to a young man from Rumania named Harris. He needed a wife and said if she married him he would pay to bring over her sisters and brother.

That was how Bessie was proposed to, and she married him.

It was a loveless marriage and they had two sons and a daughter.

Harris bought land in Brooklyn and opened an auto junk yard and scrap metal business in the roaring twenties.

He specialized in used Duisenberg automobiles. They were the speedsters of their time with v-12 engines.

Harris built a building on one of his lots that served as a garage. Next to the garage was an empty lot that he used for display of used cars and for storing scrap.

In the basement of his building he would take the engines from the Duisenberg's, rebuild them, and sell them to bootleggers who would install them in speedboats. This enabled the bootleggers to outrun the Coast Guard when they were smuggling in illegal liquor. He also liked good Scotch whisky and they always thanked him with some.

Bessie was left with the task of raising the kids, keeping house, and doing the market shopping.

Harris when he wasn't working would take vacations without her, by himself, in the Catskill Mountains.

This went on for years.

He started a major Jewish cemetery in New Jersey and put his brother-in-law Julian in charge to run it. When Julian's wife complained to him that her husband should get more money, he sold it.

When his sons couldn't get a decent job he opened a new scrap metal business in Brownsville after the war. His sons were his responsibility, Anna was her husband's.

Finally in the late nineteen fifties he had a heart attack and needed care. The doctor said he should spend time in Florida away from stress. He needed Bessie to go with him. She refused. Now it was her time to get even.

But her daughter begged her to go and she went only as long as her daughter and her family could go also.

Bessie loved her children, but her daughter Anna was close to her, as a daughter should be. So when Anna had a son, he was the light of Bessie's eye. She brought him to elementary school, fed him lunch every day, and doted on him. She had other grandchildren that she loved, but this one was special.

Harris' grandsons from his sons were the apple of Harris's eye, not Anna's son.

In nineteen sixty one Bessie suffered a major heart attack.

The family was called in to see her for one last time. They paid their respects.

When Anna's son kissed her on the cheek, she took his face with all her strength, and kissed him back. He was the only one she did this to.

Then she died.

It is suggested that after each story you _wait_ a moment or so and think about the people you just read about before going on. Thank you.

69 – The Draft

Seymour knew what was in the letter even before he opened it. He was expecting to be notified to come in for his pre-induction physical by the draft board. This was it.

In 1968 the Vietnam War was raging. Soon he would probably be there. Fighting in a jungle war was not what he wanted to do with his life.

In 1961 he was in his second year of high school and in social studies class Mrs. Kelly was showing the front page of the Herald Tribune. It told of how President Kennedy was sending advisers to South Vietnam to help out. She said it was a war and we should be aware of it.

The Second World War lasted four years or so and he figured by the time he finished high school and college it would be over. That would be seven years at least. Boy was he wrong.

Seymour had finished college and was engaged to be married. The letter said he had to report to Fort Hamilton in Brooklyn for a physical.

On the appointed day he walked through the gates to Fort Hamilton and past the MP's stationed at the gate of the fort, with old cannons overlooking the Verrazano Narrows, along with a bunch of other young men.

He had never seen a live soldier before.

Unlike news stories carried on television about other countries, New York City was under civilian control and there were no armed troops patrolling Times Square or the highways and train stations. He felt he was transported to another world.

Once inside he was sent to a large room with a hundred other young men and given a written aptitude test. The sergeant told them to do their best. Once you signed your name, you past the test so do your best, it will determine where you are placed in the army.

One hippie looking fellow took out red tape from a sack he carried and placed a red x on the floor where he was sitting. Then he placed some hay over it and pronounced to everyone that this marked that he was there.

Seymour was in total disbelief. This was weird.

After the test he had to give a urine sample in a room with the rest of the men. He couldn't go so he asked a big guy standing next to him to fill his container. He did.

Seymour had a friend who was told to say he was gay and that he wouldn't be drafted because of that. He followed his friend's instructions and asked to see the psychologist. He was told to act ashamed and not flamboyant and say that he was embarrassed to be gay. It worked and he was never drafted. The army didn't draft gay men.

Some of his college friends went to Canada to avoid the draft, he stayed. He was engaged to be married and Canada was too cold. He had relatives in Regina and they used to tell him about snow reaching their second story windows.

Now they were to get in a final line to find out if they passed the physical. Ahead of Seymour was a young gypsy with a belly that stood about two feet out from his frame. When the Captain sitting there told him he was four F he had the biggest grin from ear to ear. That's when Seymour realized he too could be four F if he ate some more.

The problem was he was only about 15 pounds away from being underweight.

It took Seymour almost forty years to get that weight on.

Now he tells people he is a recovering anorexic.

It is suggested that after each story you *wait* a moment or so and think about the people you just read about before going on. Thank you.

70 - The Actress

At fifty she was alone in her dressing room thinking back on her career in show business.

The silence in the room was punctuated by the music drifting in from the stage through the air vents. Sitting at her makeup table she remembered when she was the young starlet who had just burst on the Broadway scene.

She had dinners at fashionable restaurants, being courted by the handsome and wealthy men who were attracted to her, because of her fame.

Now she was older, had been through two marriages, and had no one to be close to as she was aging.

Although she was still an attractive woman the lines on her face were showing, her body starting to sag in the wrong places, and she was tired.

The two shows a day had become a burden to her. Her legs were not as agile as before. The dance moves she once did with spirit are now done with determination and drudgery. Her torso was stiff even though she warmed up properly as she had always done.

This play was in a small off Broadway theatre and it was written by a retired accountant who was financing it.

The director was an old flame who knew she was available and remembered her when her star was burning brightly. She still had a recognizable name in the New York theatre business but was not sought after as before. She went from top billing to barely being named on the posters outside the theatre.

Lonely and depressed she wondered where she had gone wrong. The money she made all those years was spent on divorce lawyers, fancy cars and apartments, and incompetent financial managers.

Her first husband was a successful Wall Street trader who wanted her to give up the stage, retire to a penthouse, and have three or four children with him. She thought about it but he was very unromantic to her except when they went out for the evening. She was his arm candy and nothing more.

She ended up with the penthouse after the divorce.

Her second husband was not a wealthy man. He was an author she had met through the business and he never made it big. He made a living but nothing more. But he was romantic, a great person to talk with on almost any subject, and he fit in with her lifestyle.

All he needed was his laptop computer. He used to travel with her all over the country when she was on the road touring. His office was his laptop so he was the perfect husband.

He was caring, concerned, and always thinking of her first.

This was her dream husband.

Then one year she was playing in Chicago in the winter and he slipped on some ice on the sidewalk. He fell hitting his head and started convulsing.

After he came out of the coma he started to get migraine headaches and his personality changed.

She couldn't live with him anymore. He became verbally abusive and couldn't stand any noise, or music. So when she divorced him she had to pay him alimony as she was, by far, the breadwinner in that marriage.

The plays faded into one another as the years passed. She did some bit parts on television, mostly walk-ons, nothing major. A few local talk shows had her on for interviews but they were few and far between. Mostly she was on when they were doing a revival and wanted to speak to an original cast member.

Depressed, she reached for her bottle of sleeping pills....

It is suggested that after each story you _wait_ a moment or so and think about the people you just read about before going on. Thank you.

71 – The Detail

He was stationed outside the presidential suite on the 35th floor of the Waldorf-Astoria when the president came walking down the hallway.

His palm rested on the handle of his holstered weapon.

John had many thoughts at that moment.

He was guarding the President of the United States. After seven years in the Secret Service it was his turn to do presidential duty.

It is thought to be an honor to have this assignment. Not everyone stayed in the service long enough to get this detail. Many left for lucrative careers in the private sector just before getting this detail.

Guarding the president was for the most part dreary work, especially if an agent had to watch over young daughters. And if they were in their college years it was much harder. They usually had to look the other way if there was a personal relationship between the child and someone of the other sex.

If one of the kids were in a café, and lit up a "funny" cigarette, it became a problem. They were to protect the kids, not be their nursemaid. So if a protected child was busted all they could do was inform the police and nothing more. It was the police officers discretion to arrest or not.

John was with the service for a long time. No one knew he was a convert to Islam. He was an American born citizen who converted later in life.

He was a tall Midwestern young man. Born and bred in Iowa he was blond and blue eyed. He was a typical stereotype of an American.

After high school he joined the marines and served for four years. The government paid for his college education when he got out and after graduation he went into local law enforcement.

But he always sought adventure and he applied to the FBI, DEA and the Secret Service. John felt that local law enforcement in Iowa was too boring.

He wanted his adrenalin to flow so he tried to join a federal agency.

The secret service kept him on his toes but he wanted more.

He was raised in a non-religious home and never had any thoughts of religion, either good or bad.

John had volunteered to help civilians rebuild a school in Afghanistan and was further exposed to Islamic teachings while there.

Although he was a patriot he was slowly being weaned towards a radical belief through the teachings of a low keyed Imam who was very personable and also an American citizen.

Unlike other law enforcement officers they do not keep the safety on their guns. If they pull out their weapons they are going to use them.

This day John was personally guarding the president while he was visiting New York City.

If he drew his gun he felt he would avenge the deaths of many of his Moslem brothers who were killed in Iraq and Afghanistan. Those were some of the thoughts that were running through his head at that moment. Did he have the nerve to do it?

But he would also bring dishonor to himself as a marine and to his family if he did.

He was very confused, conflicted emotionally and began sweating profusely.

If he drew his gun he could kill the president, or kill himself as a suicide.

He had choices.

But there was another choice he could make.

John turned to his partner, said he quit, handed over his gun and walked away.

Nobody died that day.

It is suggested that after each story you *wait* a moment or so and think about the people you just read about before going on. Thank you.

72 - Phyllis

She was born with a club foot and blind in one eye.

Her mother was a drug addict, lived on the streets as a prostitute, and after the birth immediately gave her up for adoption. Unfortunately she never tried to prearrange the adoption so the state placed the infant in a foster home.

As a special needs baby she was passed over many times for adoption and became a ward of the state.

She was a thin girl, tall, bright, but hyper active. The doctors thought it was due to her mother's addiction while being pregnant and the drugs affected the fetus.

Phyllis went to whatever local school was nearby the current foster home she was in. It was not unusual for her to be in a different school every other year.

When she entered high school she volunteered to help the coach with the girls track team. With her club foot she couldn't run at all. But she was cheerful and very helpful. Her hype activity helped her keep up with her duties as she never tired. She finally had a family in her teammates.

Her coach took a liking to her and told her about a new shoe she had read about. An orthopedic surgeon had just designed a shoe to enable people with a club foot to walk normally.

The coach spoke to the doctor and asked if he would build a custom sneaker for Philly at a reduced price as an experiment. The PTA offered to defray some of the cost and the team members held a car wash and other fund raising activities to help pay for it.

She was elated to finally be able to walk normally.

Once she put on the sneakers she started to walk with a normal gait.

The coach started her on an exercise routine and she started to build muscle and strengthen her legs.

Every morning she came in early to school and worked out in the gym before classes started. After school she went to the YMCA and learned to swim. This built up her stamina and her breathing.

This routine went on for almost a year.

On weekends when no one was around she went to the school track and ran the oval. Phyllis started slowly at first, then faster, until she had a gait that suited her.

When running her hype activity kicked in and she was able to run without getting as tired as some of the other girls eventually would.

Finally she asked the coach if she could jog with the other girls when they warmed up.

He thought it was okay and told her to warm up with the squad. But if she felt she was getting tired when they jogged the oval it was okay if she stopped. She said she understood.

But he had no knowledge of her extra workouts and water training.

The team lined up and started to jog slowly around the first turn. As they entered the first straight run their competitive spirits kicked in. They picked up speed. Philly stayed with the pack.

At the third turn they were in full run mode dashing for the finish line.

Sweat was dripping, their lungs grasping for air. Muscles were burning and arms and legs running in rhythm.

Then Coach had noticed that Phyllis had been keeping up with them.

As they made the final turn, saw the finish line, Phyllis sprinted and left them behind.

Coach had previously put in adoption papers for her and now she finally had a home, a family, and a future in track.

It is suggested that after each story you *wait* a moment or so and think about the people you just read about before going on. Thank you.

73 - Brooklyn

It was quiet and I was standing in the middle of my store when I saw a rusty old station wagon park across the street. The door opened and a heavy set man got out, straightened up with difficulty, and grabbed his two chrome crutches and stood there for a moment. With a jerky movement he crossed the street to stop in and say hello.

I recognized him as Sal the upholsterer. He had a small shop that my father used to send me to pick up finished goods. It was a small place under the elevated subway on the other side of Brooklyn.

Sal was older, about fortyish, and was involved with the boys.

My father told me that once he was sitting in a bar and the police came in and arrested him. They found stolen property in his locked station wagon. He claimed he had no idea how it got there.

When I saw him walk I knew he was kneecapped. He had to really tick someone off for that to happen.

But that was Brooklyn in the sixties.

There were a number of mafia crime families and you didn't mess with them.

The local police precincts were well aware of who was who. And they knew what businesses they were running. Either in the back or downstairs there was gabling and prostitutes. But the local police where on the pad and nothing happened.

I had a fellow who did our over runs when my truck was overbooked or I didn't want to send it to certain neighborhoods. He worked for me on a per job basis while he was taking thousands of dollars for the bookies to their bank. No one messed with him.

Once he had done a delivery for me and was taking the elevator down to the lobby. It was an old building and there were two doors. The inside door would open first, and then you had to push the exterior door, to exit the elevator. He saw through the glass on the door two men waiting on either side of the elevator door.

He felt they were going to mug him.

So he pushed the door open with such force that it swung open and hit one guy in the face and he collapsed to the floor. He had wrapped the cord from his drill around his hand and with a quick over the head movement hit the second one. He then calmly walked out of the building and left the two would be muggers on the floor.

When he told me about the incident I asked him how he knew they were going to mug him.

He said his friends used to do that when they were growing up. He knew what was coming.

He grew up in the Red Hook part of Brooklyn and was the only one of his friends not to go to prison.

I asked him how that happened he said they were doing too much "stuff" and he told them stop for a while. So the next time they didn't tell him and left him out of the loop. They got caught and all of them went to prison except for one guy.

When his friends got out of prison that one fellow had a very bad accident and fell down a flight of stairs and broke both legs and arms. He told me you have to be careful on stairways.

You never knew who you were dealing with in Brooklyn. You always kept your mouth closed and were respectful.

Everybody knew somebody.

It is suggested that after each story you *wait* a moment or so and think about the people you just read about before going on. Thank you.

74 - The Other Woman

Jane was now homeless. She had nowhere to live anymore and her husband had left her for a younger woman.

After years of being almost truly faithful to him she was left with nothing. She was a tall brunette who still had a very good figure. The hours spent in the gym were not wasted. Her long wavy hair was past her shoulders and when she went out men's heads turned and noticed her. But now she had to do something.

He got the house by bribing the judge in their divorce case and then cleaned out their joint bank account of all their savings.

She found out about the affair from a "friend" who was in Europe on business and saw her husband there with another woman. When the friend got back he immediately told Miss Jane in hopes she would leave her husband and live with him. But it didn't work out that way.

Her husband had started divorce proceedings before he left for Europe so he wouldn't be contacted by her when she was served divorce papers. But the papers weren't served before he arrived back in the states.

She knew where he worked and immediately drove to his office and stormed in to confront him.

The receptionist, Tracy, was his girlfriend. She saw her coming in and quickly told him so he had time to prepare for her. Tracy was 21, thin, had short blond hair and gray eyes that pierced into your soul when you looked at her. Tracy was mesmerizing, unbelievably beautiful, very spunky and fun to be with.

Jane opened the door to his office and slammed it shut. She took out a handgun and pointed it at him. "How can you do this to me" she demanded. He told her he didn't love her anymore and was in love with his receptionist.

Devastated she suddenly felt a surge of anger and shot him. As he fell behind his desk the receptionist, upon hearing the shot, ran in.

"Tracy" Jane screamed, "How could you do this to me? You betrayed me. We had something true between us. How could you sleep with my husband?"

Tracy stood there in disbelief. Here was her male lover lying on the floor with a gunshot wound and her secret lover holding the gun.

Instinctively she grabbed the gun away from Miss Jane and ran to the phone to call an ambulance.

"He is my baby's father" Tracy yelled at Miss Jane. "Look what you did to him. How am I going to raise my unborn child if his father dies? Why couldn't you just talk it out like a normal person?"

Miss Jane had a flashback to when she was once young and had to give up her child. She was single and her lover was a married man who refused to leave his wife. She was in the hospital and had just delivered a baby daughter. Her parents were standing by her bedside telling her she was doing the right thing by giving up the baby. Her daughter would be raised by a loving family who could care for her.

When the police came they took Tracy's information and Jane then found out Tracy's last name. She was her long lost daughter that she gave away for adoption. She was stunned and confused.

Tracy, now realizing who Jane really was, started to cry uncontrollably.

"Cut" yelled the director. "Great scene, everyone go home and we'll continue tomorrow where we left off. Cable television soaps are the best! We may even get an Emmy for this one."

It is suggested that after each story you *wait* a moment or so and think about the people you just read about before going on. Thank you.

75 – Unrequited

It was his first day in this business class. He needed some elective classes so he would have enough to graduate and go to college. This seemed like an easy way to kill some credits.

The teacher looked as bored as he was. It must have been his 20 something year of teaching the same class. He didn't even have to look at his notes, or the class. He just stared out the window and talked in a boring monotone.

Just when Michael was about to start closing his eyes in walked a clone of a young Mary Tyler Moore. Her name was Fran and she even wore her hair in a flip just like Mary. He was smitten. She was very cute and petite.

She made eye contact with him and after class he went over to her and started a small conversation. She was a junior and she only took business classes, not academic to prep for college. But at seventeen Michael wasn't interested in her brains.

In high school he had joined a fraternity and was assigned a "big brother". Paul was two years older and in college. He was very tall, smoked a pipe (to look distinguished) and took him on double dates with sorority girls he met.

Being busy with his band and playing in the school orchestra Michael just flirted with Fran and never had the time to ask her out. Then about three weeks after they met she came over and told him that he knew her boyfriend, Paul.

They were going steady and had been together for over two years. As she spoke about him Michael could see that she was crazy about Paul and he had no chance to go out with her.

He was now in a bind. Does he tell her that Paul was dating other girls, and double dating with him, or keep silent. If he told her Paul was cheating would she then go out with him, he thought not. In ancient times they always killed the messenger of bad news, so why chance it. It was would be a long time until he finally had the opportunity to tell her.

It must have been fifteen years later and Michael was working in retail when Fran came in, by chance, to make a purchase. She was a little older looking, crow's feet by her eyes, but still cute. Not as effervescent as in high school but that was due to her divorce.

She told him she was not with Paul anymore because she caught him cheating (that was old news to him). Michael told her he was sorry to hear it, and that she was left with a child and no support. Paul was a dead beat dad.

It was then that he told her he was crazy about her in high school.

She asked why he didn't ask her out, she said she would have gone. But Michael realized that she was speaking as a divorced woman and not as a love struck teenager.

He told her that she never would have gone out with him then.

Michael nicely reminded her she was in love with Paul and really would not have dated anyone else. He must have hit a nerve as her eyes welled up, her smile drooped a little, and she agreed with him.

He would have asked her out at that moment but was now married, with kids, and was not about to jeopardize his marriage. What could have been…?

And he still thought she looked like Mary Tyler Moore.

It is suggested that after each story you *wait* a moment or so and think about the people you just read about before going on. Thank you.

www.ingramcontent.com/pod-product-compliance
Lightning Source LLC
LaVergne TN
LVHW051604070426
835507LV00021B/2761